SUPPORT
AND
SEDUCTION

SUPPORT
AND
SEDUCTION

The History of Corsets and Bras

By Béatrice Fontanel

Translated from the French by Willard Wood

Harry N. Abrams, Inc., Publishers

CONTENTS

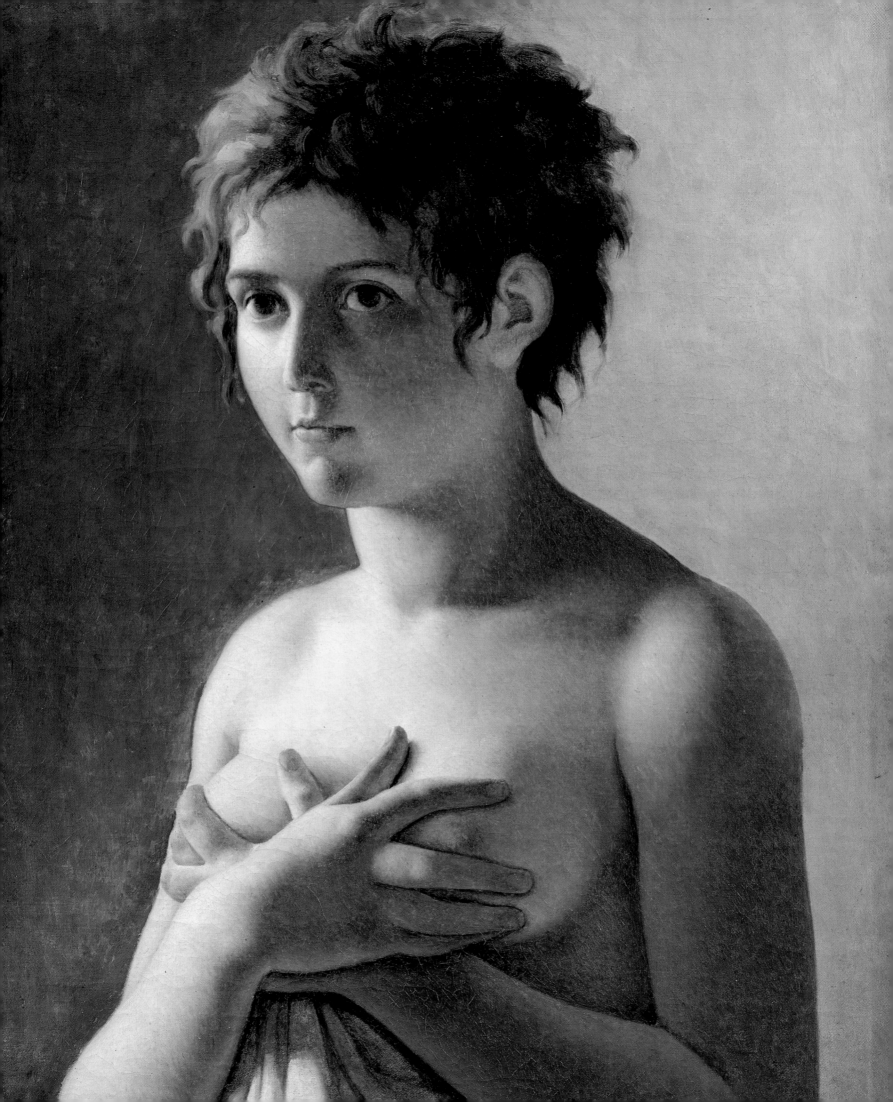

"On the soft wax of the human body, each society stamps its impress."

Philippe Perrot

Compressed, uplifted, flattened, made to jut out, left *au naturel*—women's breasts have lived through many incarnations. After centuries of corsets that squeezed their breasts, bruised their waists, sheathed their bodies in armor, and made them all the more desirable, women finally jettisoned this instrument of torture at the beginning of the twentieth century for an item of clothing that was just as complicated but much less constricting—the brassiere.

At the dawn of prehistory, "civilized" man sought to distinguish himself from animals and "savages," who lived naked and allowed their sexual organs to sag with age. The birth of modesty no doubt contributed to the invention of underclothes, as did the love of seduction—hiding and revealing what one wants to show—and the nostalgia for youth. The ancient Greeks felt as women do today that flaccid, bobbing breasts are unattractive and uncomfortable. In the intervening centuries, the aesthetics of the breast have fluctuated dramatically.

BRAS OF ANTIQUITY

Cretan "décolletages," Roman "two-pieces." . . . What was worn under classical draperies? One of the first décolletages in the history of human-kind was also one of the boldest. At the start of the second millennium B.C., the women of Crete wore a corset that supported their breasts at the base and thrust them outward, spectacular and naked. This feminine ideal is embodied in the Snake Goddess, a polychromed terra-cotta statuette representing a woman wearing heavy face paint and baring large, protuberant breasts. Though the goddess rises to us from the depths of time, she still haunts the modern male imagination. The art historian Elie Faure, writing at the beginning of the century, was probably considering her when he described Cretan women as "painted and unnatural dolls—bare-breasted, with reddened lips and black-encircled eyes, wearing flounced dresses in barbaric bad taste." The French scholar Jacques Laurent (also known as Cecil Saint Laurent), in his history of female under-garments, chastised Faure for his moralizing attitude: "Their outright sensuality would turn them into dolls only in the

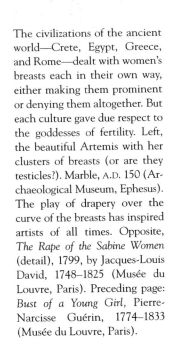

The civilizations of the ancient world—Crete, Egypt, Greece, and Rome—dealt with women's breasts each in their own way, either making them prominent or denying them altogether. But each culture gave due respect to the goddesses of fertility. Left, the beautiful Artemis with her clusters of breasts (or are they testicles?). Marble, A.D. 150 (Ar-chaeological Museum, Ephesus). The play of drapery over the curve of the breasts has inspired artists of all times. Opposite, *The Rape of the Sabine Women* (detail), 1799, by Jacques-Louis David, 1748–1825 (Musée du Louvre, Paris). Preceding page: *Bust of a Young Girl*, Pierre-Narcisse Guérin, 1774–1833 (Musée du Louvre, Paris).

eyes of a Lutheran." For his part, he preferred to fantasize: "The Cretan female, lush-fleshed and whetted by her swollen underclothes, by her garish flounces, the make-up garish on her face, evinces a violent desire to seduce—an awesome bitch." These learned men, with their contradictory views, project the sensibility of a twentieth-century male on a woman of 2000 B.C. In fact, Cretan women were far from being sexual objects and played a primary role in society. They participated fully with men in the capture of bulls and the running of nautical expeditions. More significantly, it was they who formed the caste of bare-breasted priestesses who officiated at the rites of the female divinities worshiped by the society as a whole. But more important still, as the Greek historian Nicolas Platon informs us, Minoan civilization was the first to aestheticize adornment and give it the status of an art form, on a par with painting and sculpture. The clothing of the Cretans is a direct precursor of twentieth-century fashion. Just as Paris in the nineteenth and twentieth centuries was a beacon for fashion all over the world, Crete played a preeminent role all over the Mediterranean. Cretan women had only to change the way they draped their loincloths for the women of Egypt and the women of Phoenicia shortly to follow suit. The Snake Goddess is not, in consequence, an arrogant temptress. She presents her breasts, like an offering of fruit, to the devotees who worship her. In her own more seductive way, she is a fertility symbol like the callipygian (large-buttocked) Venuses of prehistory. A high-ranking Egyptian

woman went about as her Cretan counterpart did with a naked bust, the only difference being that her breasts did not swell out from the pressure of a corset. She wore a fluid, transparent dress that tied quite naturally below her breasts. Her servants went entirely naked, or wore a loincloth.

The proto-bra appeared with the rise of Greek civilization. During the archaic period, around 1000 B.C., women began wearing the *apodesme*, a strip of cloth, often red in color, that they wore rolled below their breasts. In the classical period of the fifth century B.C., it became a wide band of cloth that wrapped around a woman's chest to lift and support her breasts. The purpose in Greece was not to make the breasts prominent, but to hold them firmly in place and prevent them from jouncing while a woman walked. This seeming modesty on the part of the Greeks can be explained by their passion for beauty and harmony. Later, the Greeks developed brassieres with slightly scary names: the *anamaskhaliter* and the *mastodeton* (from *mastos*, breast), which were again bands of cloth that bound the breasts.*

In the early days of the Roman Empire, women also wore bandages, called *fascia*, which cinched the breasts and were intended to slow their growth. If nature won out and a woman's breasts developed to an

The word "mastodon," coined in 1806 by Georges Cuvier, is a composite of mastos *and* odontos, *tooth, and describes the nipple-shaped protuberances on the molars of these large, extinct pachyderms.*

The Cretans venerated the Snake Goddess, opposite left, as the great earth-deity, c. 1600 B.C. (Palace of Knossos, Crete). Opposite right, the Venus of Willendorf (Musée de l'Homme, Paris). The earliest known sculptures, dating back more than 25,000 years, are female figurines. Left, the lady Toui. Egyptian figurine (Musée du Louvre, Paris). Below, the goddess Thoueris, a female hippopotamus with fat flanks, a fertility symbol. Egyptian figurine (British Museum, London). Overleaf, two female athletes train with weights and the discus. Unlike the Greeks, the Romans did not practice nudity in the gymnasium. Chamber of the Ten Maidens, detail of a mosaic from a villa (Piazza Armerina, Sicily).

exaggerated size, she might have recourse to the *mamillare*, a soft leather bra that squashed the matron's bosom—and may have accounted for her proverbial ill humor, according to the fashion historian Maguelonne Toussaint-Samat. In fact, only women whose breasts were truly overdeveloped wore them. Another option was the *strophium*, a sort of scarf that enfolded one's breasts and gave them support without compressing them.

History records that at least once these strips of cloth were put to more tragic use. In his *Annals* (A.D. 65), Tacitus tells the story of Piso's conspiracy against Nero. When a courtesan, Epicharis, was implicated in the plot and tortured, she strangled herself using her *fascia*.

The Roman state, envisioning itself as the lance-bearer of civilization, had little tolerance for soft mammae and despised so-called barbarian women, whose breasts hung and swayed. Strange concoctions existed to prevent the breasts from developing too much. The botanist-physician Dioscorides counseled women to apply the powdered stone of Naxos to their *fascia*. Pliny prescribed the use of grinder's mud. Ovid suggested poultices of soft bread crumbs dipped in milk. What these surprising recipes reveal plainly enough is that Roman women were expected to efface their female attributes—and that they labored under a status inferior to men. The behavior of these "little creatures," as some Roman authors called them, held little interest for the exclusively male world of politicians. The historian Peter Brown writes that prominent Romans tended to impose a strict puritanical code on their wives, who were bound by traditional strictures, much as one finds in Islamic countries today. Among the people, however, these rigid principles had little currency, and they had even less among the barbarians. With the fall of the Roman Empire and the great invasions of the Celts and Germans, the practice of binding the breasts fell into disuse. Barbarian women left their breasts free under a tunic or dress, just as Christian women did in the early Middle Ages and continued to do for several centuries. Only in the Gothic period, when clothes that mold the body again came into fashion, were breasts bound once more.

A system of crossed ribbons worn over the tunic—somewhat in the manner of the Playtex "Cross Your Heart" bra—supports the breasts of these Roman women. Opposite, *The Baths at Caracalla*, by Sir Lawrence Alma-Tadema, 1836–1912 (private collection). Below, the goddess Isis, the "consoling mother," a marble statue from Pompeii (National Museum, Naples). Roman women also used breast wrappings, which they wore under their togas and did not remove even when they made love, apparently. Paintings from the brothels of Pompeii show women naked except for their bras, suggesting that it was more taboo to show one's breasts than one's buttocks.

nent auoir ensemble ses seuures sir

ido la noble phema
enne. laquelle furt
premierement pr nom
appellee elisse en la

MEDIEVAL BREASTS, SMALL AND MOLDED

After the end of Greco-Roman antiquity, the main task of fashion was seemingly to hide the human form, compressing the breasts with bandages and draping the body with voluminous clothes. But during the twelfth and thirteenth centuries, clothes were again used to give the body definition. Slenderness and verticality were emphasized. Clothing clung to the body and was tailored to lengthen one's line. Women came to resemble narrow Gothic columns.

While the ancients focused little attention on the breasts, certain authors of the Middle Ages, to judge from their texts, found the thought of them troubling, especially small ones, white and firm. It must be said, however, that the men of that era were just as given to fantasizing about a well-rounded stomach, the tip of a foot, or the outline of a woman's calf.

Now that fitted garments were in style, master tailors evolved, each jealously guarding the secrets of his manufacture. A variety of models were offered, lacing up in front, behind, or even to the side, but all tailored to fit closely to the body: there was the *cotte*, a laced tunic that certain historians of fashion have identified as an ancestor of the corset; the *bliaunt*, a sort of bodice, laced in the back or on the side, that molded the bust like a

The idealized female physique of the Middle Ages consisted of small breasts and a rounded stomach. Opposite, Dido, queen of Carthage, from a fifteenth-century manuscript of *Concerning Famous Women* by Giovanni Boccaccio, 1313–1375 (Condé Museum, Chantilly). Left, Eve, from *Adoration of the Mystic Lamb* (the *Ghent Altarpiece*), a multi-panel work by Hubert and Jan van Eyck completed in 1432 (Church of St. Bavo, Ghent).

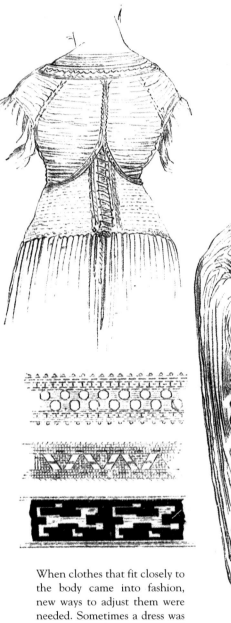

When clothes that fit closely to the body came into fashion, new ways to adjust them were needed. Sometimes a dress was sewn on in the morning and unstitched at night. Lacings and buttons also underwent a great period of development. Above and right, the *bliaunt* (Bibliothèque des Arts Décoratifs, Paris).

breastplate and was sewn to a pleated skirt; the *sorquerie*, a close-fitting *cotte* that was also called a *wardecorps* or corset; and the *surcot*, a bodice that was slipped on over the dress and laced. The latter would remain in fashion until the Renaissance, first laced behind, then laced in front. All these garments hugged the breasts tightly, to the point of making them disappear. Bandages to hold in the breasts came back into fashion for a time. They were worn over the shift. In the medieval *Romance of the Rose*, the author suggests, "And if her paps be too heavy, let her bind her breast with cloth."

The Christian puritanism of the Middle Ages, taking up where Roman virtue had left off, took care that the new sartorial liberties should not lead to excess. In the twelfth century small bells were all the rage. They were worn at the belt and along the neckline (these must be the only jingling breasts in history). In Germany, an edict issued by the Nuremberg municipal council forbade the wearing of bells by men or women.

In the thirteenth century, the décolletage was hidden behind a triangle of cloth, generally black. The Church was willing, on the whole, to forgive women for adopting the

PLVS EST EN VOVS GRVTVSE

PLVS EST · EN VOVS · GRVTVSE

new style of low-cut neckline, but railed vehemently against women whose dresses were too short. The foot and, worse yet, the calf were far more erotically charged than the breast. Yet the longer women's trains grew, the deeper plunged their necklines. A knight by the name of de La Tour Landry, a literate country squire, writing a manual for the education of young girls (1371–72), wondered what could possibly be the use of inordinately long trains, which gather mud "like the hole of an ewe, soiled behind," and are absurd inasmuch as "women suffer terrible cold to their bellies and breasts, which are in much greater need of warmth than their heels." Despite the disapproval of the

Noblewomen at a tournament wearing fashions from Burgundy, late fifteenth century. From Albert Racinet's *Histoire du costume*, 1888 (Bibliothèque des Arts Décoratifs, Paris). So extravagant was women's attire at times—V-shaped necklines that were often trimmed with fur, embroidered "hennins," or steeple headdresses—that Franciscan monks refused absolution to women who wore trains of undue length.

19

devout, women found sly ways to get around prohibitions. The black breast kerchief, for instance, was tailored of transparent cloth, allowing the lines of the throat to be glimpsed.

At the end of the Middle Ages, the human form began to come into its own. Yet young women retained a measured outlook, only "uncovering the shoulders to a greater or a less extent, and veiling or revealing the hair and cleavage; the high-necked guimpe, the wimple, handkerchiefs, and lace were among the delicate and alluring defenses interposed between the public and the intimate," wrote historian Philippe Braunstein in the *History of Private Life*.

In the fifteenth century, the Duchy of Burgundy was one of the richest and most powerful in Europe. Burgundian fashions influenced all the European courts. Women wore a wide belt below the bust, designed to support the base of the breasts and lift them like apples. They dragged a long graceful train behind them and a veil that often touched the ground. The typical gown, deeply scooped at the neckline, was matched with an extravagant headdress, whose tall conical shape could be two feet in height.

This getup gave women a strange silhouette, with their breasts unusually high. Sometimes they wore a close-fitting vest or gilet that flattened the breasts and emphasized their globular stomachs, an effect they achieved by slipping a stuffed sack under their clothes. In an era when Europe was sparsely populated, the womb-stomach was often disproportionately large—presumably this, too, was a fertility symbol. Isabeau of Bavaria, queen of France, was the first to wear the décolletage, "that smile of the bodice." Revealing one's cleavage became more and more fashionable, to the point where men of the cloth raised a terrible outcry. The Czech reformer Jan Hus roundly condemned "those women who wear gowns so deeply and so widely cut at the neckline that fully half the breast is exposed, so that their bursting flesh may be seen anywhere and by all, at the temple

before the priests and clergy, at the market, and especially at home. The covered part of the breast is so emphasized, so artificially swelled and made prominent that it resembles two horns." Elsewhere he writes that "[these same horns] are lifted very high and artificially projected forward, even where nature has not supplied women with such large endowments; at last, thanks to the shape of the bodice and an excess of clothing, the horns of their breast rise upward."

OUT OF THE BLUE, THE BREAST OF AGNES SOREL

Difficult times—the Black Plague of 1348, which killed a third of Europe's population, and the Hundred Years War (1337–1453)—were followed by a stable and prosperous period during which people could taste the pleasures of life.

"In no other period of the past was the beauty of the female body so represented or exalted as during [the Renaissance] . . . when the erotic was glorified all over Europe," explains Jean Delumeau in his history of the Renaissance. He takes as an example a painting by Lucas Cranach that shows Venus draped in transparent veils.

A painting by the French painter and miniaturist Jean Fouquet (c. 1420–c. 1481), a *Virgin and Child*, depicts a noblewoman with one breast uncovered. The model was most likely Agnès Sorel, Charles VII's mistress and the first royal favorite in the history of France. Artists at the time were fond of scenes of surprise indiscretion, in the vein of the Fouquet painting. Beautiful and

The queen of fashion at the court of Charles VII was Agnès Sorel. Belts were high and tight, necklines set off with velvet. Opposite, *The Virgin of Melun* from the famous Melun Diptych by Jean Fouquet (Musée des Beaux-Arts, Anvers). Above, a portrait of Agnès Sorel (Loches Château).

23

From the fifteenth century on, the eroticism of a woman attending to her body was a commonplace. The many portraits of women interrupted at their toilet show them surrounded by objects to make themselves beautiful—pearl necklaces, combs, mirrors. Right, Diane de Poitiers, the mistress of Henri II (a man nineteen years her junior) and later of his father, François I. School of Fontainebleau (Basel). Opposite, Saint Mary Magdalene in an elegant dress. Her sleeve of brocaded damask, with its pattern of flowers and strawberries, is held by a pin to the tightly laced bodice. At the neckline can be seen a fine linen shirt. Detail from the right panel of the Braque Triptych by Rogier van der Weyden, 1399/1400–1464 (Musée du Louvre, Paris).

intelligent, Sorel played an important political role despite her short life—she died at age twenty-eight—and exerted a salutary influence on the king, who was by nature indolent. It was she who encouraged him to help Joan of Arc battle the English.

A century later, an anonymous painter portrayed Agnès Sorel in the same pose, but minus the infant Christ. This sixteenth-century artist may have gotten wind of the rumor that Sorel launched the extravagant fashion of one breast in, one breast out. This unexpected dishevelment, writes Jean-Claude Bologne, was particularly erotic since it gave the impression of undressing. Though the nuance is subtle, the artist's muse displayed the unveiling of the breast, rather than an unveiled breast.

Poets were also immersed in the general climate of sensuality, as these lines from John Donne's "To His Mistress Going to Bed" show:

Off with that girdle, like heaven's zone glistering,
But a far fairer world encompassing.
Unpin that spangled breastplate that you wear,
That the eyes of busy fools may be stopped there.
Unlace yourself, for that harmonious chime,
Tells me from you that now it is bed time.
Off with that happy busk, which I envy,
That still can be and still can stand so nigh.
Your gown going off, such beauteous state reveals,
As when from flowery meads the hill's shadow steals.

The breasts, which the men of the fifteenth century had so adulated, were still supported, as they had been in the Middle Ages, by an external garment. In the course of time, this item of dress would grow heavier and more rigid. The basquine, which derived from the medieval *cottes* and *surcots*, consisted of a tight-fitting sleeveless bodice worn over a shirt and laced at the back. To stiffen it, the basquine was lined with prepared cloth,

and even reinforced with brass wire. Here, too, some historians of dress have seen an ancestor to the corset.

As the dress of men became shorter and less cumbersome, a decided difference began to declare itself between the costume of men and women. Women's dress sheathed their upper body, narrowed their waists, and lengthened their silhouette by adding a train, which kept a woman's ankles and calves hidden should she happen to bend down. The logic had its flaws, as one could then look down her front. These dresses, which added on behind what they lost in the front, were mocked by the French preacher Michel Menot, who imagined the following dialogue between a man and his wife:

"Madam, since all the world may look on your bare breasts, what is to prevent them from seeing all the rest?"

"What would you have me do, sir, as my dress is tailored in this fashion?"

"Remove a piece from your train, which is far too long, and put it on your bosom where cloth is lacking."

The woman then takes up the scissors, tears off her dress, and throws it at her husband, saying: "I believe you would play at being a tailor, cut it as you please."

This little farce was played out in pantomime by Menot, for the amusement of his

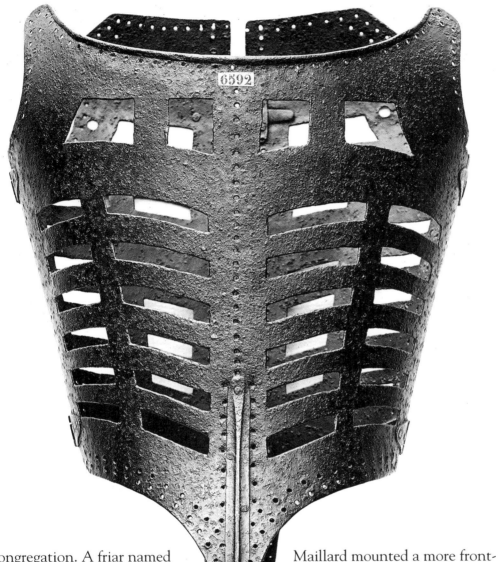

6592

Women's costume, which until the sixteenth century was simply close-fitting, began to grow more and more rigid. Opposite, Jane Seymour, third wife of King Henry VIII, with her bust compressed into a funnel shape by a dress of heavy fabric, embroidered with gold thread. The wide, square-cut neckline echoes the geometry of the headdress; large sleeves give the figure its majestic stature. The sitter's social prominence is clearly indicated by the fabrics and jewels, which are depicted with extraordinary precision. Detail of a painting on wood from 1536 by Hans Holbein the Younger (Kuntshistorisches Museum, Vienna). Left, iron bodice, fifteenth century (Musée de Cluny, Paris). These extraordinary metal cages were worn only by women with physical deformities.

congregation. A friar named al assault, apostrophizing the gentlewomen who wear open your husbands every time they did not hesitate to address, women of the congregation. swept over Europe did not arise Maillard mounted a more frontwomen in his church: "You dresses, are you not cuckolding lead you to the banquets?" He sometimes by name, certain Yet the waves of moralism that by chance. They were not provoked by a few pure spirits but often followed on the heels of syphilis epidemics, which struck terror in the hearts of all.

27

FROM STIFFNESS TO VIRTUE

At the end of the Renaissance, male and female costume became ever darker and more rigid. Spain, whose empire dominated Europe under Charles V, set the fashion. Gone were the rounded back, slight chest, narrow hips, potbelly, and sinuous lines of the Middle Ages; in their place came a new sensibility that prized rectitude. A turn toward a somewhat haughty bearing is noticeable. In order to be fashionable, a woman of nobility had to be virtuous (just as in the eighteenth century a certain degree of libertinism was in good taste). The new restrictions were adopted at court, where they served to bolster both the courtiers' bodies and their souls against the uncertainties of the times. It was the close, in fact, of a period of internal peace and humanist *joie de vivre* and the start of the religious tensions between Catholics and Protestants that would soon lead to a regimen of killing and terror.

Under the reign of Henri II in the mid-sixteenth century, the padded silhouette came into being, with its flat stomach, narrow waist, and bust in the shape of a cone. A strip of rigid material, the busk, was slid down the front of the corset. Made of boxwood, ivory, engraved mother-of-pearl, damascened silver—

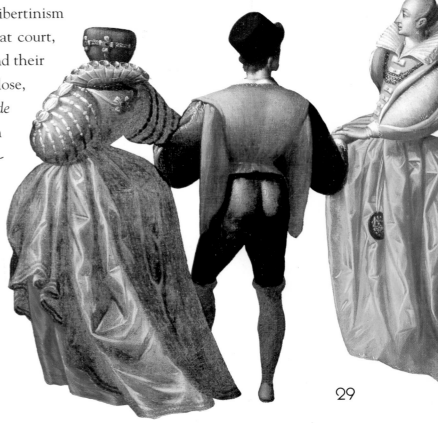

For a time women were deprived of their low-cut necklines. Their austere dress included high-necked gowns and heavy ruffs, sometimes so wide that they were forced to eat with a long-handled spoon. Opposite, a painting by the Dutch portraitist Thomas de Keyser, 1596–1667. Below, *Ball at the Court of Henri II*, detail, French school, second half of the sixteenth century (Musée du Louvre, Paris).

29

or, among the less wealthy, of turkey cartilage—the busk sometimes held a dagger. When one had eaten too much, it was always possible to remove the busk from the slot sewn for it in the bodice and show it around, which explains the fashion for highly wrought and valuable busks. Some carried finely engraved inscriptions, such as this unusual homage, which is written as though spoken by the busk:

I have from Madam this grace
that I may rest long on her bosom,
from where I heard a lover sigh
that he would well take my place.

So violently did these straitjackets deform the body that the more enlightened minds were alarmed. Ambroise Paré, who was considered the father of modern surgery and was the personal physician of Henri II, François II, Charles IX, and Henri III, found himself one day confronted on his dissecting table with the cadaver of a narrow-waisted woman. He was thus able to show his students the effects of masking women's breasts: his subject's ribs overlapped one another.

Women's busts were henceforth to remain prisoners, despite all changes of fashion. The dark dresses of the Spanish style, high-necked and topped by a cartwheel ruff, gave way to the wide-collared décolletages brought into fashion by Queen Marie de Médicis, wife of Henri IV.

In the seventeenth century, France was still not a stable kingdom. The king was constantly at war with his nobles. After the civil insurrection of the Fronde in 1648, the French government became more authoritarian and imposed on the court a heavier and more solemn demeanor. The desire to court absolute power is evident in the châteaux, gardens, and clothing of the period. Classicism was at its height, and Catholicism triumphant. At mid-century, the government kept free-thinkers under surveillance; the more sanctimonious elements of society spoke out against actors and condemned public dances.

Cardinal Mazarin, who managed affairs of state during the minority of Louis XIV, issued edicts in 1644 and 1656 against gold and silver trimmings and accessories to female dress.

How did women manage to have those funnel-shaped busts? Thanks to the busk, several of which appear opposite, suspended like swords of Damocles above the head of Ambroise Paré. Engraving (Bibliothèque Nationale, Paris). Below, Marie de Médicis, wife of Henri IV. Engraving (Bibliothèque des Arts Décoratifs, Paris).

In fact, these proclamations were aimed at lowering the nobles' pride a peg or two. The following anecdote provides a good illustration of the puritanism of Louis XIII: one day the king, who could not abide the fashion for low-cut dresses, spat a mouthful of wine onto the exposed bosom of a lady at court.

During the reign of Louis XIV, the low neckline was hidden under a fichu, a triangular scarf of a fine, transparent linen, carelessly thrown on around the neck. The *gourgandine*, with its evocative name, was a laced corset, partly open in front. The pretty little bows on either side of the breasts, designed to hide a fastening, were known by various gallant names. The king's mistress, Mme de Montespan, brought loose-fitting gowns into fashion to hide her numerous pregnancies (she had eight children by the king), and corsets lost in popularity. When she fell from favor, however, corsets made a triumphant return. They proved extremely practical for supporting one's back during the long ceremonies a courtier was expected to attend, sometimes standing for several hours.

Until September 7, 1675, only tailors had the right to make corsets. But as moralists attacked licentious behavior with mounting force (numerous caricatures of the period show tailors groping their clients on the pretext of taking their measurements), Parliament authorized seamstresses to form a corporation of their own to compete with tailors. This was to have a significant effect, as the new breed of corset-makers was naturally more sensitive to a woman's concerns and applied themselves to making corsets that were lighter and less painful to wear.

The same year, a work was published by the abbé Jacques Boileau (brother of the famous poet Nicolas Boileau-Despréaux) entitled *On the Nudity of the Throat and Its Abuses*. In the course of eighty pages, the author recounts his horror of

women who wear décolletage: "Let us try at least to imitate the zeal of Saint John Chrysostom. . . . Let us inform these women, as he did, of their great fault in coming to church wearing indecent clothes and, if I may say, partly naked. Do you come to the house of God as to a ball, the great man would ask them, do you come to this place of worship to win hearts and gratify your sensual nature? . . . Must we make a bed for you? Know you not that you will be carried here in a coffin to feed the worms?

"If we may not yet prevent this nudity, alas, let us make our disapproval of it plain by averting our gaze from it. . . . For to look at a fine breast may be as fatal as to look on the basilisk."

Sermons against "the nudity of the throat" rang out all through the seventeenth century. The sin was venial and could be atoned for with a few Our Fathers. If the

Tailor's costume, opposite. Engraving (Bibliothèque des Arts Décoratifs, Paris). Seamstresses obtained the right to create a guild of their own in 1675, arguing that it was "advantageous to the well-being of women and girls, and befitting their modesty, to be dressed by persons of their own sex." Below, detail from *The Fair Reader*, pastel, Jean-Etienne Liotard, 1702–1789 (Rijksmuseum, Amsterdam).

décolletage had gone too far, a good spanking, administered by the father confessor behind the altar, might rectify the situation. In a treatise on slovenly dress, one author debates the question of whether a woman who wears a low-cut dress commits a venial or a mortal sin. The answer, it turns out, depends on the depth and width of the transgression, and on the number of people who have witnessed it. But there are aggravating circumstances, such as if one catches a cold in the winter because of one's undress—is not a death resulting from the exposure of too much flesh a form of suicide? What damns a woman above all else, however, is to wear a cross between her breasts. Rather she should wear an image of a toad or a crow, creatures "who take pleasure in filth."

By contrast with this astonishingly violent text, Tartuffe's observation in Molière's play ("Hide this breast, I would not look upon it") seems quite mild, if just as hypocritical. Yet the queen mother, Anne of Austria, a woman who practiced her devotions faithfully, was shocked by it when she saw the play. In fact, *Tartuffe* was banned for a time and the public forbidden to see it, though the play was thought a highly entertaining one.

The ladies at court were in any case well punished for their vanity. The corset put too much pressure against the stomach and compressed the solar plexus to the point where women fainted at the drop of a hat, particularly after meals. If women had the vapors, therefore, it was not entirely out of coquetry. When women had fainting spells they were given smelling salts, but more importantly their lacings were loosened. An advertising slogan for a corset, displayed in the window of a corset-maker's shop, gives some idea of the bawdy humor of the times: "Contains the strong, sustains the weak, brings back those who have strayed."

Under the influence of the philosophers, the hysteria of religious bigots gradually gave way to rationality. Men and women of the upper classes could now live and think more freely.

Opposite, Saint John Chrysostom, patriarch of Constantinople, who in the fourth century A.D. preached famously against luxury and adultery. He singled out for censure the empress Eudoxia, whose love of pomp and splendor scandalized the Christian population. In 403, she obtained her antagonist's exile. *Saint John Chrysostom Preaching before the Empress Eudoxia*, c. 1880, Joseph Wencker (Crozatier Museum, Le Puy-en-Velay, France). Above, portrait of Anne of Austria by Pierre Mignard, 1612–1695 (Musée de Versailles).

BARE BREASTS OF THE REVOLUTION

After lying on his deathbed for an eternity, Louis XIV died in 1715. Morals had never been so strict as during the last years of his reign. The Regency period that followed, under Philippe d'Orléans, saw society suddenly set free. One no longer heard murderous polemics on the nudity of the breast. Freethinkers began to speak out, and necklines again dipped lower. The elegant society of the salons was ruled by women—it was they who directed conversation, they who supported the intellectuals, and their influence extended even to politics and the economy. As expressed by the historian André Bourde: "Whether at Versailles or in the gardens of the Palais Royal, in the salons or the dressmaker's shop, the women of that century were more than an ornament to society, they were its motivating force."

Aristocratic ladies of the eighteenth century played at the princess and the pea. In fact, they had to be very strong to endure the torture caused by their corsets. Above, *La Duchesse de Talleyrand*, engraving after Elisabeth Vigée-Lebrun, 1755–1842. Right, *Madame de Pompadour*, engraving after François Boucher, 1703–1770. Below, eighteenth-century bodices. The one on the left was for nursing women. Opposite, detail from *Kitchen Interior*, Joachim Beuckelaer, c. 1530–c. 1573.

Women's minds cast off their shackles during the eighteenth century, yet their upper bodies were held compressed by their corsets. The use of whalebone stays, more flexible and form-fitting than the busk, made corsets far less rigid. And as the skirts of women's dresses were also extended by whalebone hoops, the demand for whalebone was considerable. The Estates General of the Netherlands, for instance, authorized a loan of 600,000 florins in June 1722 to support the Dutch whale-fishing season in the North Sea.

By the end of the eighteenth century, whalebone stays had supplanted the central busk. The boned corset no longer served to mask the breasts, but instead compressed them from below to make them bulge upward—the nipples always seemed on the verge of popping out. The inside of the corset, of unbleached cotton, was fairly rough, while the outside was of damask, satin, or embroidered or brocaded silk. Certain corset-makers created veritable works of art and poetry, such as a bodice of pink ribbed silk, or faille, trimmed in white kid and reinforced with reeds.

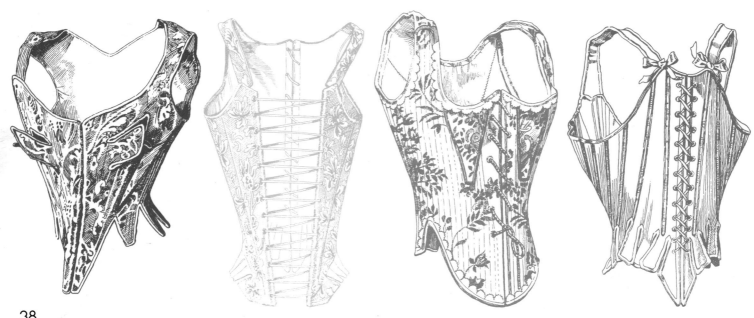

One wonders why, from the sixteenth to the late nineteenth century, the corset was never challenged by the women of the aristocracy or the bourgeoisie. The reason may have been that it served first and foremost as a sign of their superiority. Those wearing it were barred from even the slightest useful exertion, thus reinforcing the prestige of the ruling class. The body, hidden under an absurd structure, offered up a stylized ideal of the human form. Women of the aristocracy felt that to wear a corset was more vital than health itself, so imperative was the need to distinguish oneself from the common people.

Women of modest means, of course, had to work. Country women wore no foundation garments, only a skirt and a shirt over which they slipped a corselet, derived from the medieval *cotte*. It was laced but not tightly, defining the waist and supporting the breasts. Corselets laced up the front, as opposed to the corsets of the aristocracy, which, lacing behind, required the assistance of a maidservant.

Even before the French Revolution, thanks to the influence of Jean-Jacques Rousseau, a general movement toward simplicity and a return to nature was felt, which extended even to the nobility. It was not uncommon for a marquise to unlace her corsets and give her child the breast, a revolutionary act. Since about 1750, the medical

Marie-Antoinette had her share of influence on post-revolutionary fashions. After the excesses of the mid-1770s—towering hairstyles, masses of ribbons and garlands—fashion took an opposite course. The queen, with her penchant for the farmwife look—lace bonnets, pastel-colored dresses—inspired a simpler silhouette. Above, *Marie-Antoinette with a Rose*, by Elisabeth Vigée-Lebrun, 1755–1842 (Château de Versailles). Right, a "breast bowl" of Sèvres porcelain made expressly for the queen, who wished to promote the virtues of milk.

profession had been crusading against the corset, and in 1770 a famous pamphlet appeared whose subject was "The Degradation of the Human Species Due to Whalebone Corsets." Rousseau himself took an active part in the anti-corset campaign. Doctors and even the celebrated naturalist Comte George-Louis Leclerc de Buffon agitated for getting rid of this "body press." The ultimate anachronism for which the waning ancien régime was accountable was the extraordinary architecture of women's dress at court: the

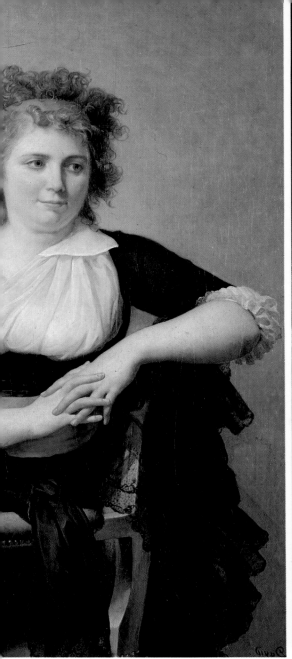

corset was shaped like an hourglass, and a small horsehair pad was attached to it at the lower back, which had the effect of projecting a woman's silhouette outward at the rear. The Revolution swept away all this sartorial armature. Boned corsets were specifically prohibited, probably because they were a symbol of the aristocracy. Clothing became simpler and more practical, and fashion reached out to other levels of the population. Women took pleasure in dressing as soubrettes, wearing a small unboned corset over a shirt, and a simple skirt.

A new style from England did a great deal to encourage the vogue for more relaxed outfits. No doubt the climate of the British Isles, visits to the colonies, life on shipboard for extended periods, and the British love of sport all contributed to the English predilection for comfortable clothes. The landed

During the French Revolution, "a great simplicity of dress, viz. worn and threadbare clothing, was considered a proof of patriotism," wrote the Englishman John Moore. In fact, the fair citizens did not abandon their coquetry altogether. They wore linen fichus with the ends crossed at the breasts or billowing blouses that amplified the bust. Above center, a portrait of Jeanne-Robertinne Rilliet, 1790, by Jacques-Louis David (Musée du Louvre, Paris). Above, *Mrs. Lowndes-Stone*, by Thomas Gainsborough, 1727–1788 (Gulbenkian Museum, Lisbon).

41

aristocracy played a dominant role in British society—they took part in the management of their own estates and were great enthusiasts of hunting and horse racing. None of these activities could be pursued in tightly fitting clothes.

In France, the great theme of the degeneration of the body was seen to go hand in hand with the degeneration of the old regime. Restraints of all sorts were to be abolished, and this applied as much to the swaddling of newborns as to corsets. Yet the rich theme of the fragility and softness of a woman's body was not to be supplanted after all. The five-pound banknotes issued by the revolutionary authorities carried the signature of a civil servant named Corset, and rakes would offer them to ladies of easy virtue saying "A Corset for a corset."

Below, *Essential Gifts for the New Year*, a caricature on wigs (Bibliothèque des Arts Décoratifs, Paris). Opposite, *The Galleries of the Palais-Royal*, where one met ladies of doubtful virtue in extremely low-cut dresses and heard talk of great frankness. Engraving by Louis-Léopold Boilly, 1761–1845 (Musée Carnavalet, Paris).

The shawl was the great fashion accessory. The trick was to have enormous ones, made of cashmere, and to wrap one's shoulders in them without hiding any part of one's décolletage. Right, *Madame Tallien*, by Jacques-Louis David.

After the severities imposed on society by the chaste Robespierre, a kind of madness came over Paris: sober gowns with kerchiefs modestly crossed over the fair citizens' bosoms were whisked away. The classical style came back into fashion. For the first time in centuries, women abandoned their hoops and padded bodices. Breasts were supported by a cloth brassiere. Women felt that it was modern to be able to fit their entire wardrobe in a single sack, and as the boned corset did not fold it was impossible to include. The fashion was for transparent cloth—muslins and tulles. The décolletages of the women of fashion, a "gauzy nudity," as it was described by Dr. Desessartz, was responsible for many pulmonary fluxes. More stylish women died in one year from such illnesses than in all the bloody days of the Reign of Terror.

Around 1795, the queen of Paris fashions was Mme Tallien, known as Our Lady of Thermidor. In the autumn of that year, she attended a ball wearing a sleeveless silk tunic with no undergarments, rings on her fingers, and sandals on her feet. Talleyrand reported that "it would have been impossible to display oneself more sumptuously." Mme Tallien, who never in her life went near a corset, attributed the youthful preservation of her charms to bathing in crushed strawberries and raspberries. Even more farfetched methods have been used at various times and in various places to maintain the beauty of the breasts. Nurses in London during the mid-eighteenth century, for instance, believed they could prevent any impairment to the breasts of new mothers by cloaking them in rabbit skins.

Yet the idea that the body needed to be firmly supported was so deeply entrenched that corsets soon reappeared. At first they were unboned, and the outer fabric was of velvet or satin. Corset tailors made every effort to adapt their wares to the changing tastes of their clientele. One of the new models, aptly illustrating the eternal vacillations of history, was known as the Ninon corset—it reintroduced boning but was cut short, ending at the waist.

At the start of the nineteenth century, a growing sense of modesty led women to avoid male specialists. The corset-making firm of Lacroix and Furet, for instance, styled themselves "surgeon-bandagers" to allay the anxieties of their clients.

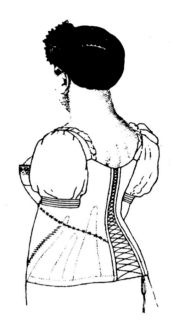

The Ninon corset of 1810, above, brought back boning to women's undergarments. It was padded below the waist to flesh out a woman's hips. Left, *The Committee for the Supervision of Morals*, a 1798 British engraving poking fun at the clergy's opposition to the skimpy dress of ballet dancers (Bibliothèque des Arts Décoratifs, Paris).

THE TRIUMPH OF
THE CORSET

The "Spécialité" Corset

In the nineteenth century, an era of great primness, the prudish bourgeoise wore high-necked dresses for daywear. Yet the décolletage still flourished in the context of the evening gown, which was ironically described as "dressy." One of the basic principles in deciding decency was the appropriateness of a particular attire to its place and circumstance. Ladies who appeared at the opera in gowns that were insufficiently low at the neckline were sometimes asked to leave their loges. Empress Eugénie in Paris and William II in Berlin could be punctilious on this score.

During the Napoleonic era (1804–15) and the Restoration (1815–30), the corset reigned despotically. The fashion was for wide-set breasts, and this acrobatic feat was accomplished with the help of a complex system of boning, invented by the corsetmaker Leroy. These corsets were known as "divorces." After the Restoration, gowns were cut with even lower décolletages. The waistline, which had ridden up to just beneath the breasts, dropped back to its normal height. This once more provoked a liking for slender silhouettes and, inevitably, brought on ever crueler corsets. Comfort again took a back seat to appearances.

At this time, corsets were still very expensive, costing from twenty to forty francs (about 140 dollars in today's currency). Women who made their own at

Nineteenth-century gentlemen bestowed unprecedented admiration on the hourglass silhouette, strangulated in a rosecolored corset. Above, a British advertisement for the "Spécialité Corset."

Opposite, *The Singer Rose Caron*, by Auguste Toulmouche, 1828–1890 (Musée Carnavalet, Paris).

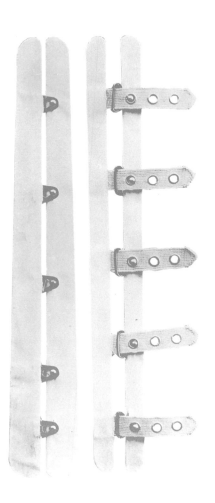

home in order to economize were advised in how-to manuals to use extremely strong and lasting cloth: bombazine, a twilled or corded dress material; nankeen from the Indies; or unbleached broadcloth.

Books that offered practical or health advice often contained elaborate theories from specialists. The following passage gives an example: "Steel busks are to be avoided as they cause electricity to gather at the bust and may occasion an internal irritation of the chest or stomach. To avoid this inconvenience, they are to be covered with gummed taffeta." As whalebone busks tended to bow outward over time, an ingenious solution was proposed: "When you notice the stays beginning to give, wear your corset inside out for several days."

While women worried over the noxious electricity produced by their readily deformed busks, King Charles X repined: "It was not uncommon in the old days to discover a Diana, a Venus, or a Niobe in France; nowadays one meets only wasps."

The romantic woman of 1830, with her full sleeves and great bell-shaped skirts—her garments, in short, a mass of swollen volumes—needed to define her waist all the more explicitly. She was transformed into a great silky insect with outspread wings.

At the Exposition Universelle of 1823, the first mechanical corset was exhibited. The corset was equipped with small pulleys, not as a specialty item for sadomasochists, but as a clever design that allowed women to lace and unlace their corsets unassisted. When Josselin, originally a merchant in braids and trimmings, observed his wife cutting her corset lace because no one was on hand to help her, he invented the Instant Release system. A line of pulleys and miniature gadgets, as precise as the workings of a clock, ran up and down the corset's back, allowing a woman to unfasten it all by herself.

Toward 1828, a discovery was made that greatly improved the strength and durability of garments, namely the inven-

tion of metal eyelets for the laces. These were much stronger than embroidered eyelets, yet hand-embroidery continued to be placed over the metal insert. Josselin, seconded by Nolet, invented the two-part busk with metal fasteners, considerably simplifying the task of hooking up one's corset. Systems for closing the garments were added on and superimposed, sometimes making corsets look like orthopedic undergarments. While there existed only two patents for corsets in 1828, sixty-four would be registered between 1828 and 1848.

In 1832, a Swiss tailor named Jean Werly established in Bar-le-Duc the first factory to weave seamless corsets. The garments emerged from the loom boned, busked, fanned out, and ready to sell. This first advance in industrialized corset-making would make it possible to put corsets on the market that were distinctly less expensive.

The year 1840 was another important date in the history of the corset. A system of lacing known as "lazy lacing" was developed. A set of elastic laces allowed a woman to dress and undress without the help of a servant, a husband, or a lover. This was a great convenience for adulterous women, as a famous caricature from this era demonstrates: a husband is surprised on helping his wife undress in the evening to find the knots on her corset different from the ones he remembers tying in the morning.

The woman of the 1840s, in her corset and crinolines, appeared spectacularly useless. The less natural her appearance, the more seductive she became.

Many caricaturists used the corset as a prop in their mockery of cuckolds. *Suspicion*, left, provides an illustration of this inexhaustible theme. Again, it is the corset that betrays the unfaithful wife: "That's funny, this morning I made an overhand knot and tonight it's a bow!" Above, box for a "Mexican" corset (Musée de la Bonneterie, Troyes).

Her body was hidden under a great quantity of fabric trimmed with ribbons and frills. Laced, fastened, and buttoned into the complexities of her dress, she simultaneously offered and withheld herself. And behind the mask of the woman's parade outfit was her body, as soft and white as could be desired.

In the mid-nineteenth century, women began to take over from tailors the specialized work of making corsets. The garments were made in lots ahead of time—this was the beginning of ready-to-wear.

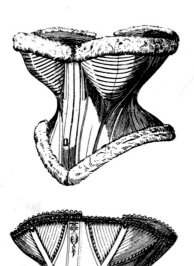

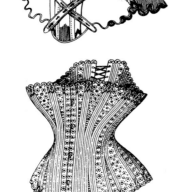

During this period the general passion for crinolines provoked unexpected tragedies. The larger the bell of the skirt, the more tightly the waist was pinched in. A Paris paper reported the following story in 1859: "A young woman, whose thin waist was admired by all her rivals, died two days after the ball. What had happened? Her family decided to find out the cause of her sudden death at such a young age and had an autopsy performed. The findings were rather surprising: the liver had been pierced by three of the girl's ribs! This shows how one may die at the age of twenty-three, not of typhus or in childbirth but because of a corset."

One particularly fervent opponent of both the crinoline and the corset was Friedrich Theodor Vischer, a professor of aesthetics: "The crinoline is impertinent by virtue of its size and its monstrous challenge to men. When a man draws near, the crinoline seems to say: 'Kindly step down from this sidewalk—or will you have the audacity to brush me in passing, to press up against me?'"

Whereas the fashionable female of the revolutionary years was long and willowy, the Second Empire woman was buxom. The corsets of those years were so long that they bruised the thighs. The fashion was for boat-necked décolletages that left the shoulders naked and the breasts low, "majestic protuberances, pale and soft, no longer made to arch upward but to be worn low, as though two pears gathered in a pair of goblets" (Philippe Perrot, *Les Dessus et les Dessous de la bourgeoisie*).

"My darling's slender waist can be encircled, I believe, by the fingers of my two hands" could well have been said of the actress Polaire, left, in 1890. But the photographs of that period were often retouched and the reality may have been less extreme. Opposite, from top: the Léoty corset, 1867; a corset from 1872 "priced at Fr 6.90 at the *Grand marché parisien*"; "a seamless corset from Bar-le-Duc, entirely embroidered and hemmed by hand"; and "a seamless corset with 54 stays, total weight 300 grams [10 oz.]" (from Léoty's *Le Corset à travers les ages*, 1893). Overleaf, *Empress Eugénie and Her Ladies of Honor*, 1855, Franz Xaver Winterhalter (Château de Compiègne). The Prussian field marshal von Moltke describes the empress as she appears in the painting: "Beautiful, elegant, with a superb throat and arms, slender in silhouette and wearing an exquisite, luxurious dress."

From the 1870s until 1914, women would remain in fetters. Over her chemise she would continue to wear a strangling corset. Fashion lost its direction, and the silhouette of women seems to have wavered. The crinoline vanished and was replaced by the combination of corsetry and bustle that gave women the typical S-bend silhouette of the turn of the century—and made them look like geese. The bust was thrust forward, overhanging the stomach, while behind a snail shell seemed to be dragged. Caricaturists were quick to notice that the new shapes gave ladies a resemblance to domestic fowl.

In the nineteenth century, corsetry reached its cruel and lunatic extremes. Models became more numerous and more specialized. Catalogues offered a wide selection: nuptial corsets, corsets made of white satin for the ball, lightly boned morning corsets, stayless corsets for night wear, nursing corsets with drawbridge gussets, traveling corsets with tabs that could be let out at night for sleeping, riding corsets with elastic at the hips; corsets for singing, for dancing, for bathing at the seaside (unboned), for riding the velocipede (made of jersey); cool and supple doeskin corsets for summer wear, pearl gray or chamois-colored and trimmed with Nile or periwinkle satin; and net corsets of violet silk cord with a small sachet of perfume hanging in the center. The many fabrics and laces made it possible to invent an infinite number of different models. A corset-maker might mix Chantilly or Valenciennes

lace with Pekin ribbon, brocaded silk with lawn (a fine linen) or Irish guipure. The constricting mechanism was now set several notches tighter. And on top of everything else, a woman had to worry, while being strangled at the waist into an hourglass, about a new, internal enemy—the rust that was eating away at her metallic stays! Luckily, the Warner Company in America had invented stays of stainless steel.

THE FOUNDATIONS OF CONTROVERSY

Comptoir des Corsets

CORSETS POUR FILLETTES

A book published in 1857 by Charles Dubois seems to summarize in its title the moral concerns of the age: *An Examination of Five Plagues: Corsets, Tobacco, Gambling, Strong Drink and Illegal Speculation.* It is true that the mothers of that era would harp at their daughters: "You'll never make a good marriage unless you pinch in your waist." Countess Drohojowska, a feminist before her time, painted a melodramatic picture of the subject: "How many instances of gastritis, of liver complaints, of migraines, of anxious or unhappy moods might not easily have been cured, at first, simply by loosening a corset lace, yet reached a stage where they were no longer curable and prematurely dug the victim's grave. The family looked on in distress when it was they, often, who by admiring women with bodies deformed by long misshaping, had encouraged the aberration." Dr. A. Debay, in his handbook on the physiology and hygiene of marriage (popular enough to go through 171 printings) argued that the corset was dangerous. A kind of medical hysteria then flared up over the corset. Some doctors held corsets responsible for all sorts of terrible damage they were unlikely to have caused: chest complaints, deformities, inability to nurse, sagging breasts, inadequate nipples. A humorist who was against the use of corsets caricatured the fate of young girls thus: "At night

One of the captions in the above advertisement for girls' corsets specifies that the Venus corset is "guaranteed to use new whalebone," suggesting that less expensive models might be made with retreaded stays. Opposite, an advertisement for the Thylda corset (Bibliothèque des Arts Décoratifs, Paris).

they are taken out of their cases, only to be slipped back into them the next day."

Other doctors were not at a loss for arguments with which to ridicule these exaggerations. A fierce proponent of the corset complained that "Just about everything is now blamed on the corset, as though the individuals involved differed only with respect to how much or how little they used corsets; and as though differences in their constitutions, their physical strength, their lifestyles, their hereditary traits, their illnesses, their race, etc. were not equally capable of providing causes for the dissimilarities between them." Another doctor, a fount of common sense, urged "the development of the muscular system by means of exercise, gymnastics, and cold baths." Still other doctors added angry voices to the fray. According to a Dr. Delmas: "No one who has admittance to one of those houses where young girls are raised under high pressure has not heard a hundred times the mother's injunction to her daughter: 'Young lady, hold yourself straight.' For the poor girl to obey she would have to be allowed outdoors to play with a skip rope or a hoop. Instead she is given a busk. She is tightly laced into a boned, steely corset that bruises her body and suffocates her. Here is what happens: when the young girl is sixteen she is hunchbacked. If she is not hunchbacked she is chlorotic, her stomach no longer functions; she huffs rather than breathes; her arms are like spindles, her legs like drumsticks...." Behind the physiological criticism are glimmers of a new social criticism addressing the unfair treatment of women.

In 1870, the majority still believed that corsets supported the

breasts and prevented the viscera from deforming the abdomen. Thanks to the corset, the internal organs stayed safely in their cavities. What nightmares are conjured up by the words of a contemporary physician: "I have often in the past heard . . . that 'every man should wear an athletic supporter.' Might we not also say that every adult woman, given a normal degree of physical development, should wear a corset, which is none other than an athletic supporter for the mammary glands, as they are just as exposed to dangerous shocks and wrenchings?"

Yet certain gentlemen would for a long time be unable to decide whether they were for or against corsets. Armand Silvestre, the author of a bawdy history of female lingerie, refers to the corset as "the happiest of prisons," and again as "a gracious instrument of torture."

Illustrations by Louis Le Riverend from Armand Silvestre's book on the history of lingerie. Undoubtedly, they are more erotic fantasies than strict depictions of historical fact. From left, a *guêpière* of forged steel, worn by a young lady from the Middle Ages, who leans nonchalantly against her spinning wheel; the "stitched bodice" of a licentious marquise, who, her breasts bare, has just finished writing an amorous letter; the typical nineteenth-century corset; and an extraordinary bodysuit which, again, bares the breasts.

I am weary of so often describing the container. Might I not devote a page to the contents, the lovely twins so many poets have sung, the glorious breasts?

Marble, satin, velvety rock
resolving this great quandary:
to be soft yet firm
How rare a quality!
Snowy heights where melts
the enemy of the steppes and lowlands
Sumptuous treasures that leave us
Innocents with full hands.

What is a good corset? Here is Silvestre's answer: "It must lace up properly, and the pressure it exerts, at all points moderate, must be abated where apply-

ing to the more sensitive and less sturdy organs. It must provide no obstacle to the movement of the ribs or abdomen in breathing nor to the ampliation of the stomach and intestine during digestion. The upper portion must be sufficiently flared to support the breasts without compressing them, and the arm-holes cut wide; the lining must be thin, correctly placed, and flexible . . . and finally, it must embrace the entire pelvis and find solid support on the hips and follow the natural direction of the flanks." He might just as well be describing a corseted cow! Nothing if not flexible, Silvestre goes on to change his mind: "In Greece, women clothed themselves for centuries without this instrument of torture. Did it make them any less pretty? Go visit Polymnia at the Louvre and tell me about it!"

Nonetheless, at the end of the nineteenth century women were so tightly corseted that they could not bend over. Worse yet, the corset was hung with an

Foundation garments with their padded accessories, right, held many surprises and required delicate adjustments that could be performed only with the help of a servant. Over their false bottoms, women added flounces, drapes, and bows. "Why this great attention to the backside during so straitlaced an era?" wonders Maguelonne Toussaint-Samat in her *Histoire technique et morale du vêtement*. This froth of ribbon and lace cascading from a slender waist and lengthening the lower back indefinitely produced a charming effect. Women ended up looking like majestic peacocks. Opposite, *The Ball*, by James Tissot, 1836–1902 (Musée d'Orsay, Paris).

extraordinary amount of gear, a combined system of garters and suspenders. The idea was to hold up the stockings, prevent them from twisting, and keep the corset tightly stretched. Getting dressed was as complicated as rigging a ship.

At the Labor Exposition of 1885, the artificial breast was introduced. It could be made of chamois leather, quilted satin, or India rubber. One model, the "Mammif," was a pair of false breasts designed to be worn in a corset, its particular interest being that it could be inflated at will! A story reported in the *Frankfurt Gazette* suggests that falsies of this type could sometimes create a sensation: "At a dinner recently given in Vienna, one lady was singled out above the others for the elegance of her figure and the perfection of her attire. In the quarter hour before dinner, she was surrounded by a swarm of admirers, one of whom was so bold as to offer her the flower from his buttonhole. The

gift was accepted, and, as the gown worn by this ravishing lady laced up behind, the flower was attached to her breast with a pin. Hardly had the guests taken their places around the table when a peculiar sound was heard, like the sighing of the south wind. When the lady's admirer turned toward her in astonishment, he was horrified to observe that the charms that had so enticed him were visibly diminishing. . . . The rounded forms had vanished by the time the soup course was half over." There were also artificial breasts with suction cups, to keep them from moving around awkwardly under one's dress. Humorists were quick to point out that not only did these false breasts enhance a woman's figure, but they could serve as a life vest in case of shipwreck.

As to real breasts, the newspapers of the period had the idea (probably for the first time in history) of conducting a survey on the topic among their readers. In 1891, the *Courrier français* asked the following indiscreet question: "Do you prefer them in the shape of apples or pears?" One reader answered with disarming sincerity: "A starving man who is offered an omelet doesn't care if it is made with truffles or asparagus spears. I am living in a hole of a village taking the country air, and I mostly do without. I'm hungry, period. And since you're applying to botany for your images, I can tell you that tonight I couldn't care if they were shaped like pears or apples, in fact, I'd be delighted to hold a pair in the vulgar shape of pumpkins, big floppy outsized ones—and be a happier man than you, no matter what you have that's better."

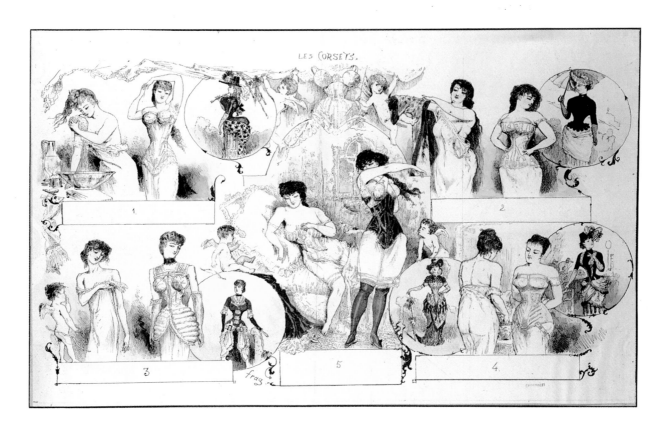

LES CORSETS.

Another reader, presumably an electrician, delivered himself of this weighty axiom: "Apples preserve their neutral fluid by virtue of their round-ness; pears discharge electricity at the pointed end." Yet fully three hun-dred gentlemen preferred apple-shaped breasts, and only thirty favored them pear-shaped.

An Agence France-Presse release, dated February 28, 1990, reports that, in a survey of five hundred women from the ages of fifteen to thirty-five, 69 percent of respondents preferred apple-shaped breasts while 27 percent pre-ferred them pear-shaped. One detail that is somewhat hard to interpret is that women in managerial positions more often chose apples while those in subor-dinate positions chose pears. What can we conclude? Nothing, unless it is that women managers in the late twentieth century have the same tastes as men of a century earlier.

"That lovely rose on your cor-sage has the most delightful smell!" exclaims the tipsy bour-geois to the young flirt, who lowers her head but swells out her bosom. Color engraving by Ferdinand von Reznicek, 1904. Above, *Corsets*, a satiric engrav-ing in *La vie parisienne*, c. 1870 (Musée Carnavalet, Paris).

In the last years of the nineteenth century, a Dr. Witkowski published a grand work in several volumes (its radical title, *Tétomania* or "Titomania," gives some indication of its tone) exploring every medical, literary, and artistic curiosity relating to the breasts, the corset, and décolletage! This erudite work gathers myriad juicy anecdotes, drawn from every imaginable realm.

From the realm of religion: "Muhammad correctly said that a woman's breasts feed the child and rejoice the father"; ethnography: "[The mammae] are useful to the newborn, as they provide him his first food, of which he is exceedingly fond; and they are agreeable to the adult, as they concur with the other female charms in exciting the senses toward the reproduction of the species"; practical tips: "[The breasts] afford the seamstress a natural pincushion by the projection of the bodice, particularly on the left side"; technology: "The space between the breasts, which the boarders at convents call the 'holy water font' (perhaps because the fingers are drawn to it?), can be used as a bouquet-holder if a woman is stout and wears a décolletage"; history: "We know that during the Directoire period, when the fashion was for clinging

gowns with no pockets, the leather purse was deposited in the intermammary crevice. In our day, it serves as a hiding place and a mailbox."

In the volume dealing with pathology, the author takes an interest in breast size. Women who lack passion have, according to him, underdeveloped breasts. The nipple may be more or less projecting; a nursemaid, he informs us, must have nipples at least the size of an average thimble. Often when it has cracked or abscessed, the nipple will retract into the breast like a finger withdrawn from a glove, leaving a navel-like aperture. This anomaly may remind us of a famous story from the *Confessions* of Jean-Jacques Rousseau, in which the author, stopping in Venice, was unable to satisfy Zulietta, after discovering that she had "a blind breast."

Mme Seurre of Paris was undoubtedly one of the first to make sports bras. The one advertised above seems to have been very sensibly tailored. Advertisements such as the one for Marguerite Lagrange's designs, above left, emphasized the importance of a good corset in preserving one's bust. It is practically considered a medication, as the ad calls it an "Infallible Treatment."

While coquettish women of the nineteenth century padded their corsets, nuns tried to hold back the invasion of too generous a bust by compressing their mammary glands behind roundels of punk. Contemporary doctors explained with straight faces that, however much one's femininity was compressed above, it reappeared below. The breasts would atrophy thanks to the iodine naturally present in punk, according to the doctors, but another development the nuns had not counted on would also occur: "Thanks to the interrelation of our organic parts, the reproductive apparatus will profit from the retraction of the mammary glands. As the pelvis is the anatomical and physiological expression of the womb, the hips and buttock muscles of women who have undergone this treatment will experience enormous development." Nuns also took water-lily powder for its apparent capacity to induce frigidity and reduce breast size—but no one has been able to specify the dosage.

Witkowski reports that the nuns of the Bon Pasteur d'Annonay convent in the Ardèche were sued and convicted by the court of Tournon after one of their boarders brought a complaint: "If our arms were not crossed on our chests while we slept, for whatever reason, we were put into a 'restraining corset' [a type of straitjacket] on the pretext that we had been doing something dirty with our hands." Finally, Witkowski describes book-loving "titomaniacs" who, horrifyingly, had their books bound in skin from women's breasts. On the covers, the nipples formed a characteristic crest. Interns from a Parisian hospital were apparently expelled for supplying breast skin to a local bookbinder. And Camille Flammarion is said to have received the macabre gift of a female admirer's upper chest skin—she was a Slavic countess who died of consumption.

Turning our attention to less fetishistic and more rational events, there was a movement at the end of the nineteenth century among a number of governments to forbid young girls from wearing corsets. In 1898, the Russian minister of public education, Bogoljewov, prohibited young girls from wearing corsets to school. The Romanian minister of education, Haret, followed suit in 1902. The same prohibition was passed in Bulgaria, applying to all state

Toward the middle of the nineteenth century, convent schools suddenly became much stricter. Young girls were expected to aspire with all their hearts to become little angels. To keep them from touching their bodies —preventing masturbation was one of the prime obsessions of the mother superior—it was thought better not to have the girls wash at all, or when they did wash not to look at themselves. The moralists of that time invested heavily in the fantasy of the virginal maiden. It would be interesting to measure the effect of this cherished dream on reality. Village girls who received a crown of roses as a sign of their exemplary virtue were obliged to prove their virginity to a doctor on the morning of the ceremony. But more forward girls indulged in competitions with their classmates over breast size. Engraving, 1793–94, by Jean-Jacques Lequeu, architect, freethinker, and revolutionary (Bibliothèque Nationale, Paris).

schools (Chichmanow edict, 1904). It is curious that these quite conservative monarchies held advanced views on corporal hygiene. Although the corset, the "satin fortress," was shaken by the siege of militant anti-corsetists, the great majority of women continued to wear corsets without a shadow of rebellion, and young boys and men continued to fantasize about this mold:

"On Sunday morning, Frédéric and Antoine would rise early and post themselves at one of the small round windows to watch the policeman's wife, bare-armed and wearing a pink corset, open the blinds on the other side of the street. Her enormous arms had the livid hue and bright pink marbling one finds on pigs' bellies. Tufts of black hair poked out from the short sleeves of her shirt. Casting a glance into the street, she leaned with both hands against the window ledge, making deep folds appear by her armpits, as great as buttock creases. What most caught the boys' fancy was the pink corset. You could not see what was inside, as it fitted over a barely open shirt. But within its projections, its resurgences, lapped in whalebone and pink fabric, the two brothers imagined a molten and voluptuous flood of mysteries, an agglutination beyond the bounds of geometry, an inexhaustible font of femininity, roiling in a fug of sweat and milking parlors" (Marcel Aymé, *La Jument verte*).

LE DERNIER CHATEAU FORT (1885)

Un distingué savant, l'éminent docteur Maréchal, vient de partir en guerre contre cet ennemi du genre humain qui s'appelle le corset, et qui reste, dans notre société moderne assoiffée d'hygiène, comme un dernier rempart de pierre que ni le temps, ni les efforts des hommes n'ont pu jeter bas. Nous devons saluer comme un héros l'éminent praticien qui engage une lutte inégale avec un adversaire...

... Qui a résisté victorieusement aux ordonnances des Rois...

... Qui s'est moqué des décrets des Empereurs...

... Qui s'est ri des excommunications des papes et des anathèmes des évêques...

... Qui a haussé les épaules aux exhortations des orateurs sacrés...

... Qui a méconnu les conseils des médecins...

... et les avis éclairés des savants et des philosophes...

... Qui n'a même pas voulu entendre la voix des peintres et des poètes...

VIVRE PRISONNIERS OU MOURIR!

... Et, à l'annonce de la nouvelle croisade, la garnison jure de mourir plutôt que d'être libre!

(COLLECTION G. AVL.)

The Cadolle Company, founded in Buenos Aires in 1887, moved to Paris in 1910. It specialized then, as it still does today, in the manufacture of custom-tailored foundation garments. Its founder, Herminie Cadolle, was a friend of Louise Michel, the famous anarchistic revolutionary, and a woman of principle, who combined leftist ideals with rather capitalistic ambitions. She left Paris to do business in Argentina, shrewdly realizing that a great boom was under way there, as was a large potential market going begging. She opened a corsetry business in Buenos Aires. Enormously active and energetic, traveling a great deal, she soon realized that the corset had become an archaic item of apparel. She was also fortunate enough to arrive at a time when it was becoming possible to use hevea rubber in the textile industry. She traveled to Lyons

The Cadolle store on the Rue Cambon, Paris, which still exists today. Opposite, cartoon by Caran d'Ache, 1885, in which the corset is compared to an impregnable fortress.

herself to encourage weavers to use this new material. The brassiere could never have been invented without elasticized fabric.

At the Exposition Universelle of 1889, Mme Cadolle displayed her first breast-girdle. Herminie's idea, which was both simple and ingenious, was to invert the source of support. The problem at hand was to support the breasts. Rather than using the hips for a fulcrum as the corset does and gathering the breasts from underneath, the new principle was to hang suspenders from the shoulders to support the breasts from above. The first order was to invent the shoulder strap. Herminie Cadolle then added elastic sections. Her first model, known as *Bien-être*, or "well-being," was not yet a simple brassiere, since it was still attached in back to a corset. But the diaphragm had finally been freed. In 1910, Herminie Cadolle came back to France to set up shop.

Today, a fifth generation of women runs the Cadolle establishment, on the Rue Cambon in Paris. This dynasty of custom-fitted corset-makers can reveal in the pages of its old account books a clientele to set one's imagination racing. Cadolle created the brassieres with secret pockets that were used by Mata Hari and the corsets worn by Cléo de Mérode, who regularly left them in the private rooms at Maxim's. One countess had her crown and family crest embroidered on her bra, while another has been using the same Cartier gold fasteners for the past thirty years. Barbara Hutton used to buy the entire collection for herself in every color. And Christina Onassis would have the same set of undergarments sent to each of her six houses.

Margaretha Geertruida Zelle, opposite, was the wife of an officer in the Dutch colonial army. She studied eastern dances in Indonesia. Once back in Europe she became a celebrated performer of Javanese and Indian dances under the name of Mata Hari. Accused of espionage on behalf of Germany during World War I, she was executed by a firing squad in 1917 outside Paris. This "dangerous spy" was in fact no more than a pathetic mythomaniac, shot for having struck a chord in the public imagination. Below, the original logo for the Cadolle establishment, with its charming old-world typography, which the company has recently revived.

DOG DAYS OF THE FIN DE SIECLE

At the Paris Exposition Universelle of 1900, the underwear exhibited at the Palace of Thread, Fabric, and Apparel caught the critics' attention: "Among the loveliest and most ravishing creations were the articles of dishabille and undergarments—seductive peignoirs, light and casual negligés, alluring petticoats, pliable and becoming corsets, along with slips, underclothes, and other accessories that skillfully mold and en-

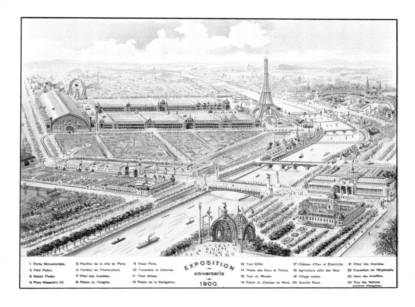

hance the silhouette, setting the imagination on fire." Also displayed to the admiration of the public were new models designed by women such as Herminie Cadolle and Dr. Gaches-Sarraute, who invented a corset that contained the belly without compressing the stomach or sides, its only drawback being that it did not support the breasts. "Women are unable to countenance leaving these pectoral tumors to their own weight," as one visitor elegantly commented. Another female doctor, a young woman named Tylicka, had devised a cloth brassiere. A Slavic designer exhibited the so-called *Callimaste*, meaning "Beauty of the Breast" in Greek. Appearing in one of the exposition's window displays, "this suspensory apparatus, applied to the bust of Diana, seemed to draw a protest from her rigid and proportionate form, which chafed

A strange and interesting portrait of a woman, opposite, painted by Gustave Courtois in 1891 (Musée d'Orsay, Paris). Mme Gauteau, the wife of a banker, was not strictly a beauty, but she is attractive with her arrogant posture, alabaster bosom, fallen strap, and very red ear. Above, a panoramic illustration of the Exposition Universelle of 1900 (Musée Carnavalet, Paris).

79

At the end of the nineteenth century, medical doctors mounted such a concerted attack against corsets that manufacturers came up with new arguments to defend them. Right, an advertisement trumpeting the virtues of the "anatomical, scientific and super-aesthetic corset of the Paris Academy," illustrated with sketches showing the effects of different corsets on the organs and skeletal structure. A British advertisement for the Specialité Corset, opposite below, makes the case that it is "manufactured according to scientific principles," and that "the shape of the stays is designed not to impede movement or respiration." Advertisement from *The Ladies' Field*, February 2, 1901.

Corset anatomique et scientifique de l'Académie de Paris

Breveté S. G. D. G.

Exécuté par Mlle E. AGIER, 22, Avenue de l'Opéra, PARIS

MEDAILLE D'OR à l'Exposition Franco-Anglaise de Londres 1908 (Première Exposition où ait figuré le "CORSET ANATOMIQUE")

Le plus grand désir de Mlle E. Agier est que chaque femme montre son corset à son docteur, à la disposition duquel elle se tiendra pour toutes explications et démonstrations qu'il pourrait désirer.

Mlle E. Agier est heureuse de signaler à sa nombreuse et fidèle clientèle sa dernière innovation, le merveilleux "Corset Gant", sans baleines ni coutures, ne se distendant jamais.

Mlle E. Agier s'engage à annuler la commande de tout corset, essayé au magasin, qui ne réunirait pas les conditions et les avantages ci-dessus décrits.

Ce corset, non seulement transforme le corps de la femme par sa forme extra-esthétique et élégante, mais il lui donne une grâce incomparable en même temps qu'une souplesse et une légèreté du corps jointe au plus grand confort. Il est construit de telle façon qu'il ne presse sur aucun organe, mais bien au contraire, la femme peut se serrer indéfiniment, sans jamais se faire du mal. La compression s'opère sur les os du bassin, au bas de l'abdomen et au bas des reins qu'il maintient en bonne position, ainsi que tout l'organisme de la femme, qui fonctionne avec aisance.

Toutes les maladies occasionnées par le port de mauvais corsets peuvent être combattues avec succès par le **Corset anatomique**.

Démonstration des avantages du Corset anatomique

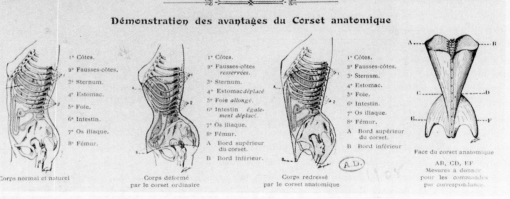

1° Côtes.	1° Côtes.	1° Côtes.	A——————B
2° Fausses-côtes.	2° Fausses-côtes *resserrées*.	2° Fausses-côtes.	
3° Sternum.	3° Sternum.	3° Sternum.	
4° Estomac.	4° Estomac *déplacé*.	4° Estomac.	
5° Foie.	5° Foie *allongé*.	5° Foie.	
6° Intestin.	6° Intestin *également déplacé*.	6° Intestin.	
7° Os iliaque.	7° Os iliaque.	7° Os iliaque.	
8° Fémur.	8° Fémur.	8° Fémur.	
	A Bord supérieur du corset.	A Bord supérieur du corset.	
	B Bord inférieur.	B Bord inférieur.	

Corps normal et naturel   Corps déformé par le corset ordinaire   Corps redressé par le corset anatomique   Face du corset anatomique

AB, CD, EF
Mesures à donner pour les commandes par correspondance.

at the humiliation of such an accessory." The exposition's lingerie section also included: the Invisible, the Ideal, the Mamellia from the Samaritaine (a Paris department store), Mme Cadolle's Breast-girdle, the Cheeky, the Expansible, the Scientific Corset, and the Scientific Health. From April to November while the exposition was in progress, women could admire these many new models, but in the heat of the summer months Parisian women tossed their corsets into the weeds.

The year 1900 marked the swan song of the corset. It lengthened, twisted, and exploded into a thousand frills, as in this advertisement: "Corset in pale blue brocaded coutil [a strong cotton fabric], strewn with white Chantilly flowerets, threaded with blue comet ribbon." In fact, it was also equipped with a long metallic rod that dug painfully and deliberately into the groin, obliging a woman to seek relief by arching her lower back—hence the overhanging bust and projecting backside. The extraordinary silhouette of women of the Belle Epoque in truth reflected the death throes of this erotic but absurd accessory.

The Ballets Russes enjoyed a phenomenal success. Their revelation of Russian art to the West in the early 1900s had an impact on every aspect of culture, even fashion. *Scheherezade* in particular, with its neo-Oriental costumes

Three photographs by the photographer Jeandel: undoubtedly one of the first stripteases ever photographed. The model, apparently a parlormaid, is shown daydreaming in her attic room fully dressed, in a corset, and finally naked (Musée d'Orsay, Paris).

February 2nd, 1901   THE LADIES' FIELD

THE "SPECIALITÉ CORSET"

IS A DREAM OF COMFORT.

Regd. Design No. 2517.

Although Paul Poiret had the mien of a senior civil servant, he was in fact a revolutionary fashion designer. He is shown here in the company of four of his models, on the occasion of a trip to London. A great admirer of the American dancer Isadora Duncan, he invited her to appear at the festivities surrounding the introduction of his new collections. Poiret was inspired by the fluid lines and oriental prints of Léon Bakst's costumes. Opposite, costume design for *Narcissus* drawn by Bakst in 1911 for Sergei Diaghilev's Ballets Russes (Fine Art Society, London).

by Léon Bakst, provided inspiration to one of the most fashionable couturiers of the day, Paul Poiret. In the United States, a movement started by Raymond Duncan and his sister Isadora brought the Greek style back into fashion. Finding success elusive in her own country, Isadora Duncan set out for Paris in 1903, where she appeared on stage barefoot and wearing only a loose tunic. She would afterward found dance schools in Berlin, then Paris.

A number of innovative fashion designers, among them Madeleine Vionnet, Nicole Groult, and especially Paul Poiret, created a new silhouette with the waist set high on the chest. Poiret revolutionized fashion by doing away with the S-bend silhouette. He brought back into favor a more natural line, which had been absent since the Directoire period. In his memoirs, he recalls those years: "It was the era of the corset. I declared war on it. The last of the rotten gadgets was a thing called the Gaches-Sarraute. Of course I have always known

women to be encumbered by their endowments and anxious to hide or distribute them. But the corset split them into two distinct masses, on the one hand the bust, throat, and breasts, on the other the entire backside; so that women seemed to be divided into two lobes and hauling a trailer. . . . It was in the name of Liberty that I advocated against the corset and in favor of the brassiere, which has gone on to become extraordinarily successful. But at the same time that I was freeing the bust, I was restricting the movement of the legs. What tears, what wailing and gnashing of teeth was caused by this fashion decree! Women complained that they could no longer walk, no longer climb into a car."

The new style in which a woman's dress restricted her lower limbs provided a bonanza for caricaturists. Madeleine Vionnet, who was perhaps inspired by the dancers Isadora Duncan and Loie Fuller, also banished the corset, had her models walk barefoot, and cut her dresses on the bias to provide more freedom of movement.

But the changes were not due simply to a handful of designers. Women themselves had evolved, and the couturiers were trying to create designs that suited them better. The lifestyle of women had changed, particularly after 1907. The haute bourgeoisie was no longer the only class to practice sports and launch new fashions; now there was a middle class of working women that was beginning to come into its own. Despite Poiret's efforts, most of them continued to wear the corset. Yet this brilliant tyrant had forbidden his clients to wear it and made a new silhouette fashionable.

The corset grew smaller and more pliable. An elegantly turned-out woman could for the first time stand up straight and be nearly free in her movements. Paradoxically, the more natural line brought on a new style of corsets that came down almost to the knees. In 1908, it was practically impossible for a woman to sit down.

English suffragettes had been campaigning against the use of corsets since 1904. An American

Isadora Duncan, opposite left, liked formless clothes in the ancient Greek style. She died in 1927, strangled when her long scarf caught in the wheel of her car. Opposite right, Loie Fuller, another great dancer, photographed by Théodore Rivière (Musée d'Orsay, Paris). This page, left and below, the corsets that were fashionable in 1913. They no longer rise as high, but they come down almost to the knees. What contortions women must have had to perform to climb the steps of a trolley car, pick something up off the ground, or even sit down.

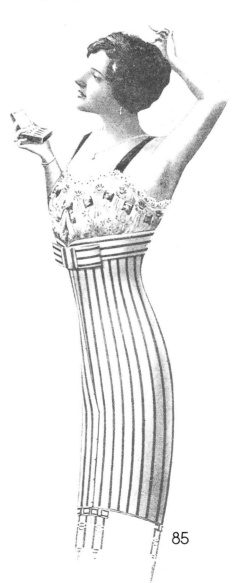

doctor named Arabelle Kenealy had made laboratory monkeys wear them to prove their debilitating effects on health and morals. In 1910, a French woman known as Mme Doria formed the League of Mothers Against the Mutilation of the Waist by Corsets. These various battles were not fought in vain, since by 1908 the structure of women's clothes had grown visibly less rigid. Women began to wear light, fluid ensembles that did not thicken their silhouettes.

In the spring of 1911, the tango became popular in America, and by the following year the vogue had spread all over the world, continuing strong until World War I. The boldness of the movements and the frenzy of the rhythm required the greatest freedom of dress. The fad for Latin American dance certainly contributed to the disappearance of the corset, and the same could be

said for certain dances from the United States—the Turkey Trot and the Bunny Hug, for example.

Yet corset-makers continued to make corsets, though those more adapted to the new lifestyles and fashions. In an account of the International Exposition of Industry and Labor held in Turin in 1911, the reporter writes, in the learned and waggish style of the day:

> The corset is certainly more sensible and less dangerous than it was sixty years ago. What is regrettable is that it strangulates the waist. Rather than being wide at the bottom, it tapers to a cone, displacing the organs and obstructing the natural functions. The radiant part, where a woman swells, and which the primitives depicted with such crude delight, should more aptly be protected. Did not the philosopher suggest that nothing in the world was more sacred, it being man's first home? . . . Corset-makers know better than any-one how the women of various Euro-pean nations are built. Each country requires a different design. The Spanish woman has a considerable stomach but no hips. . . . The Englishwoman on the contrary is straight and plans to stay straight, and she requires a corset arched from top to bottom. . . . Dutch and German

women need corsets that contain them. The average female waist in Paris measures 56 to 58 cm [22 to 23 inches], apparently smaller than elsewhere. . . . The corset as it existed in 1770, with the busk extending down the whole torso like an iron bar, and the Restoration corset with pulleys cannot be compared to the modern one, which is as supple as a glove and weighs barely 200 grams [seven ounces]. Large corset factories make every type imaginable, from corsets in coarse coutil for country women to damasked silk and brocaded satin, etc.

In 1870, four thousand Parisian women worked as corset-makers. The total production of corsets in France was 1.5 million a year. The salaries of these workers were very low, perhaps six to eight francs a day for the privileged few who worked for a large corset-maker, and as little as one and a half francs for women who worked at home or in prison workhouses. "We were shown several lovely little pink corsets fashioned by a young woman in Clermont prison, detained for strangling her two children," a visitor to the Turin exhibition reports. The same account declares that the technological superiority of the United States was already overwhelming. A piece of American equipment, for instance, could make finished eyelets ten times faster than any previous machine. And another improved the rate fivefold. Instead of punching each of the sixteen to eighteen eyelets on a side one by one, the new machine stamped out the entire set simultaneously, holing the fabric and inserting the copper rings in a single operation. The corset was then sized by being dipped in a special starch solution. The lace, embroidery, and other frills were added next. Lastly it was placed on a heated mold and the boning given its final form.

The first decade of the twentieth century saw another important advance in the textile industry. The technology of dyes improved to the point where colors could be made wash-resistant. The great wardrobe where a woman kept her trousseau was now more likely than not to contain fabrics in many hues.

Sports, particularly the bicycle riding popular in the 1910s, had the effect of encouraging women to wear jersey corsets, which did not restrict the move-

The old saying "Discomfort drives out pleasure" cannot be entirely accurate, since the fetishists of the first part of this century plainly believed complexity to be an integral aspect of a woman's attire. The getup pictured here is patently uncomfortable: the petticoat is bunched together and wedged into the garters.

ment of their legs. The pharisees, of course, considered it improper for a woman to sit astride a bicycle. Worse was the appearance of the scooped neckline around 1913, amusingly called the "pneumonia blouse" by those hidebound moralists.

In the United States, meanwhile, the design of the brassiere reached an important milestone when Mary Phelps Jacob, better known by her glamorous alias of Caresse Crosby, invented a new type of bra—very soft, short, and designed to divide the breasts in a natural way. As a young woman living in New York in 1913, she rebelled against the whalebone corset and sat down with her French housemaid to make a sort of bra that kept the breasts nicely separate using two handkerchiefs and some ribbon for babies' wear. Later her friends persuaded her to make copies of it for them as well. In November 1914, she applied for a patent and tried to market the bras commercially, but the enterprise failed and she lost a great deal of money. She then married a millionaire and sold her patent to the Warner Company. Caresse Crosby had invented the modern bra—light, simple, and fitting over the breasts. She had the good fortune to live a long life (she died in 1970) and therefore saw some of the innumerable developments of the bra.

The other side of the coin of women's luxury lingerie: it was made by unskilled workers, often from orphanages, who received just pennies an hour for ten hours' work per day. The photograph shows that by the beginning of the century, garment-making was almost exclusively the province of female workers.

THE GREAT WAR AGAINST THE CORSET

Their hands covered in engine oil and working to the point of exhaustion—labor laws had been relaxed—women would pay dearly for the emancipation brought by World War I. Opposite, a woman in an armament factory in 1916. Above, women working in a powder mill, turning out shells night and day.

World War I was to prove fatal to the corset. While the men were at the front, women did the field work, drove delivery trucks, and, out in the working-class suburbs, labored in the factories. Everywhere men had been conscripted into the army and had left their posts, and the women had filled them.

These new responsibilities also brought women new freedoms. At the beginning of the hostilities, skirts were still so long that they hampered women's movements, and corsets were a tremendous nuisance when trying to get anything done; during the war years, hems gradually rose a centimeter at a time, and corsets became smaller. Female employment in the war factories also reduced the numbers of household servants. Deprived of her chambermaid, the bourgeoise abandoned her complicated outfits and undergarments, which were in questionable taste anyway when so many wives were becoming widows. No more endless constricting layers that thickened the silhouette! A light slip tended to replace all the many items of lingerie. All in all, female underclothes grew simpler. In 1914 a new style was born that reduced volume in favor of a new freedom of appearance. Clothes were less richly ornamented, but the latest developments in the textile indus-

Nurses, known as "white angels," bring bread to the soldiers embarking for the front. These women, who were often volunteers from high society, showed great devotion to the cause. From the very start of the war, a large number of women enrolled in the Red Cross. Corsets and frills were far from their thoughts, as we can see. Opposite, a couple perform the Turkey Trot, a rather comical dance that would have a considerable run in the 1920s.

try brought into fashion such fabrics as matte and shiny satins. And the fact that lace was now produced on industrial looms put it within reach of a large number of women for the first time.

During the war years, corsets grew shorter and more pliable until at last they were replaced by the girdle. There was never a question, naturally, of forgoing all clothing that constricted the body. But the transformation of the corset into a girdle that rode lower on the body presented a technical problem—the corset might have strangled the waist, but it also supported the breasts. A shirt could be worn under the corset and snugged down to hold the chest in perfectly, but with the girdle this method of containing the breasts was no longer possible. A new accessory that had first made its appearance in the lingerie advertisements of the late nineteenth century under various names now became a virtual necessity and began to find a place in the underwear drawer of the Western woman. It was the bra, which existed already in a variety of forms, but which had never previously caught the attention of women generally. As the corset gradually disappeared, the bra became the indispensable companion to the short corset or girdle.

In 1916, women wore fairly severe, functional clothing in the daytime and at work, but at night those who had the means slipped into rather risqué dresses. Adapting to daily life in wartime was a problem each solved in his or her own way, but two principles were widely acknowledged: the need for efficiency at work and for letting off steam afterward. Décolletages became more daring, and dresses were cut from light chiffons. Women with bare backs and shoulders shimmied a Charleston on the dance floor or stepped to a lascivious tango. This taste for the seductive, which seems somewhat shocking when so many soldiers were dying at Verdun, reflects an irrepressible desire to make the most of life—one's days might, after all, be numbered. Sixty

"On the fourth of July [1918], the parading of American troops down from the Place du Trocadéro was followed with feverish excitement. The boulevards were thronged with Allied uniforms, and soldiers sat shoulder to shoulder on the terrace of the Café de la Paix or at Harry's Bar on the Rue Daunou, among our French air force aces, whose decorations swept the floor," writes Olivier Merlin in his biography of Tristan Bernard. Right, the terrace of the Café de la Paix, from the magazine *L'Illustration*.

miles from the front, ladies in feather-trimmed hats strolled the wide boulevards of Paris. The soldier who arrived in Paris on leave, the trenches and their vermin temporarily behind him, found his way at nightfall to the Place de l'Opéra and the Café de la Paix, which teemed with officers and fashionably attired women. This image of women in low-cut dresses dancing while the war dragged on depicts the period as cruel and unjust, but in fact the war was responsible for a great intermingling of the classes. Fashion made rapid inroads among women of the lower bourgeoisie, factory workers and salesgirls, though in France it still did not extend to women in the country, who constituted more than half the female population of that nation.

The policewoman made her appearance in England in 1917. By the following year, more and more Englishwomen were wearing uniforms. In France, female tram conductors wore the regulation cap and uniform jacket. Taking

their cue, a few avant-garde women began to dress in the soldier style. American women were particularly patriotic and responded to a call from the War Industries Board to stop buying steel-boned corsets, thus saving 28,000 tons of metal in 1917, the year the United States entered the war—enough to build two battleships! Others went to France to tend the wounded. "Whether in the ambulance corps or on nursing staffs, American women created a sensation by their modern aspect," Florence Montreynaud explains in her history of twentieth-century women. "They go out without chaperones, they smoke, their hair is short and permed. In feminine hygiene, they are innovative, using cotton batting for their periods and not encumbering themselves with cloth bandages [as Frenchwomen would do until the 1960s]."

Since the Middle Ages, fashion had emphasized the physical differences between men and women. For the first time this was no longer true. The

Many British and American women joined the war effort in Europe, often staffing risky stations near the war zone. Certain American millionairesses, Anne Morgan among them, contributed their fortunes for funds to help the wounded, while others financed refugee shelters or orphanages. Many received the French Legion of Honor. Above, Mrs. Harley, director of the Scottish Women's Hospital, established during the war in the abbey at Royaumont, where 10,000 wounded were treated.

LA BRASSIÈRE RÉDUCTRICE **JUNON**

BREVETÉ S. G. D. G.

EST SPÉCIALEMENT INDIQUÉE POUR LA MODE ACTUELLE QUI DEMANDE DES LIGNES SOBRES ET UN BUSTE PEU PROÉMINENT. ELLE EST DONC INDISPENSABLE AUX DAMES FORTES. ELLE GANTE PARFAITEMENT LA POITRINE ET LA RAMÈNE A DES PROPORTIONS JUSTES ET A SA PLACE NORMALE. ELLE EST TRÈS SOUPLE, NE PRODUIT AUCUNE GÊNE NI DANS LES MOUVEMENTS NI DANS LA RESPIRATION. ELLE FORME EN MÊME TEMPS UN EXCELLENT SOUTIEN FACILE A METTRE ET INSOUPÇONNABLE.

TOUT EN TRICOT SIMILI BLANC SEULEMENT

Pour contours de poitrine jusqu'à 115 c/m. Nº 702. .. .. **16 fr.** pièce.
pour contours de poitrine au-dessus de 115 c/m. Nº 703 .. .. **18·50** pièce.

EN VENTE DANS LES GRANDS MAGASINS OU BONNES MAISONS DE CORSETS OU FRANCO CONTRE MANDAT ADRESSÉ A L'INVENTEUR

JUNON, 1, Rue Ambroise-Thomas, **PARIS**

(Rayon K)

war had unexpectedly emancipated women. While men firmly invited them to return to the fireside and make babies, an urgent job after the demographic plunge of World War I, some women rebelled. Their rebellion took the form of cutting their hair short, smoking cigarettes, and wearing pants or revealing clothes. For the flapper of the twenties, it was out of the question to display a generous bosom. She wore a special bra that flattened her breasts, somewhat in the style of the Romans. This one-piece undergarment, a sort of bandeau that attached in the back, had two small tabs at the sides. Heavy lace was gone, and light fabrics replaced it—lawns and crepes. Fashionable underclothes were white, black, cream, or pink. There were also bras that did not shape the breasts but were cut loosely, giving the chest a somewhat formless look. These could sometimes be quite sophisticated—made of silk jersey, for example, with plumed butterfly motifs or multicolored silk embroidery.

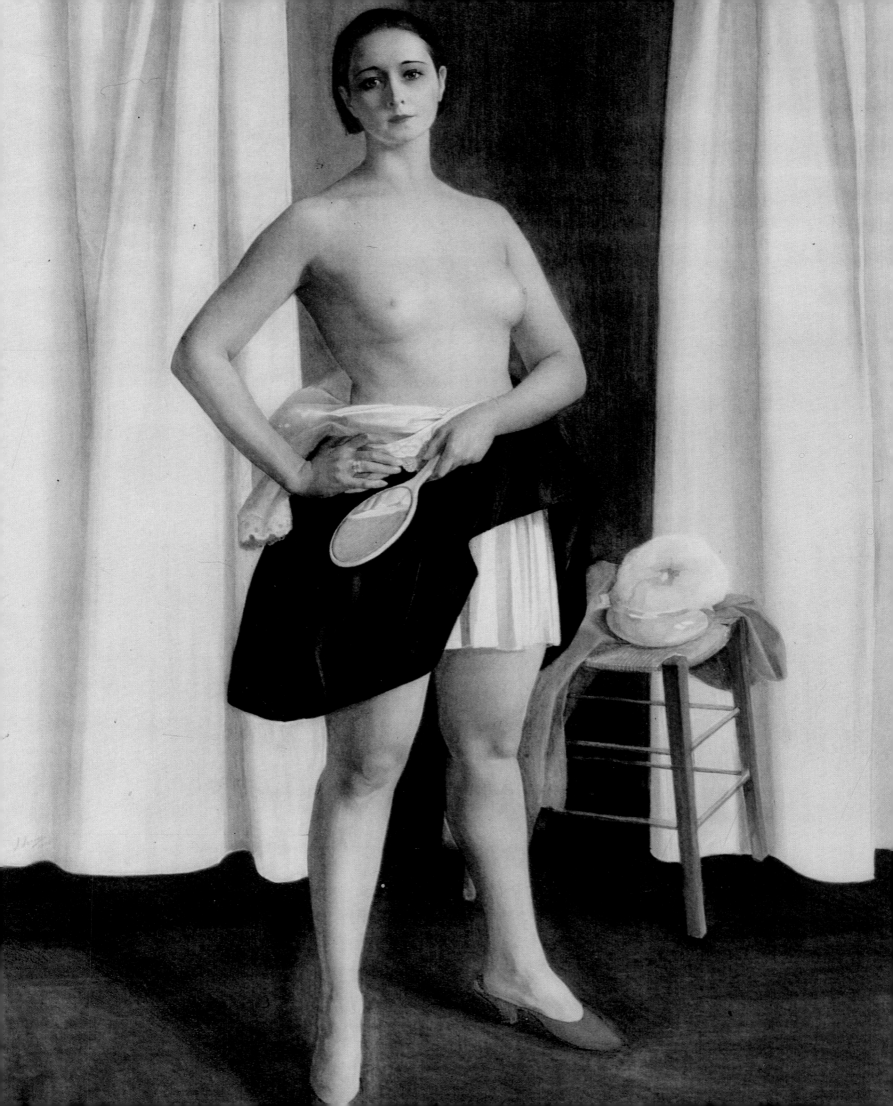

Paris nightlife was hectic, and the theaters and music halls were never empty. The whirl included operettas, the fox-trot, jazz, waltzes, the tango, and the samba. Exoticism was in fashion and one might happily have swapped a Lanvin gown for a Tuareg outfit or a caryatid's drapery, under which a corset was utterly useless. Right, *The Excelsior Cabaret*, 1929, by Joseph Mompou (private collection, Barcelona).

In the 1920s, corset-makers all turned to producing bras. Yet while there was a general vogue for flat chests, fashion magazines such as *L'Illustration* still carried a fair number of advertisements for breast-enhancement treatments.

After World War I, the dance craze took off. Dance halls and bars sprang up like mushrooms everywhere, and the whole world popped and jittered at the first strains of a jazz orchestra. Dancers were packed into halls so tightly that only their backs showed, so dresses were cut low in back. With sleeveless and low-cut dresses came a new aesthetic: women now removed their underarm hair. Legs were becoming more visible and were also depilated, and eyebrows were plucked. The ideal woman of this period was Greta Garbo, with her smooth body, perfect features, flat silhouette, and deep voice.

The concept of coordinated underclothes was also introduced in the 1920s: matching girdle, petticoat, panties, bra, slip, and corset. Prices were still high in comparison with those of today, but all the fabrics were of good quality, the garments were made by hand, and they were available in a great variety of colors: pink, light blue, mauve, peach, coral, ivory, champagne, indigo, cyclamen, apple green, jade, and black. This state of affairs would continue until World War II.

The flapper style fell out of favor in the 1930s. "No more flat chests," announced a new French fashion magazine, *Votre Beauté*. The styles created by the designers of the period suggest a softer and more feminine woman. The bias-cut dresses of Madeleine Vionnet and draped forms of Alix, the future Mme Grès, flowed freely as a woman moved.

Advertisements for brassieres (at the time, they looked more like corselets) and corsets from the Printemps department store in Paris, where one could buy, for example: "A corset in fine pink satin coutil, Fr 29, with a cup-shaped brassiere in pink sueded jersey, Fr 12.90," left, or, below from left, "a brassiere of Greek tulle, Fr 10.75, buttoned in front and laced in the back; a brassiere of broderie anglaise with a band for controlling the stomach, Fr 13.90; a heavy cotton brassiere, Fr 6.90; another bra of Greek tulle; another of broderie anglaise; and finally "a percale brassiere, along Empire lines, economically priced at Fr 4.90."

Soutien-gorge 1669
Ceinture " Moins que rien " 1004

Scandale

ADVANCES IN TECHNOLOGY

In the years before World War I, pretty underclothes were a luxury not available to all women. But a new synthetic fiber was being developed that would revolutionize the textile industry, particularly the lingerie sector. Its name was rayon, so called because of its reflective quality. Its earliest appearance can be traced back to 1883, when the English chemist Sir Joseph Swan was looking for an improved carbon filament to use in light bulbs. He discovered one and patented it, but in the end did not continue his research. His wife eventually found the cellulose fibers and decided to use them for her crochet work. The first synthetic fabric was thus a product of chance.

The crucial step in the development of rayon was taken in 1889 by the French chemist and industrialist Hilaire Bernigaud, Comte de Chardonnet de Grange, who exhibited the first articles of rayon clothing at the Exposition Universelle in Paris, describing them as artificial silk. He was able to obtain financing and start a manufacturing company in Besançon, and is considered the founder of the synthetic textile industry. In England, three chemists named Cross, Beaven, and Beadle patented another form of rayon that was to be extremely successful, viscose rayon. Production on a large scale began in England in 1905.

Advances in technology—the invention of synthetic fibers and of elastic yarn in particular—led to a new generation of undergarments, including the bra and girdle. Opposite, an advertisement for a classic of its type.

103

During the 1930s, manufacturers studied the basic kinds of bra. Its role, henceforth, was to contain and separate the breasts (Bibliothèque des Arts Décoratifs, Paris).

In real terms, rayon only came into widespread use in the twenties. It was to democratize lingerie considerably, as an appearance of luxury was for the first time available to women of modest means. A housewife with little spending money could afford lingerie that looked like silk or satin. She could now dress in soft, seductive, pastel-colored underclothes, previously available only in luxury boutiques.

Starting in 1926, the modern concept of the bra began to take shape. Manufacturers tried to make designs that supported and conformed naturally to the breasts, separating them. Rosalind Klin, director of the Kestos Company, conducted research on how to make a bra out of two handkerchiefs, somewhat as Caresse Crosby had done. She folded them and laid them across each other, then assembled them in one piece with a divider between them. For years the name of this design was synonymous with "bra"—one did not buy a "bra" but a "Kestos." Once designs began to separate the breasts, the bra underwent a good number of further improvements.

The 1930s were extraordinary years for corsetry. The materials changed, and the designs and methods of construction as well. But the fruit of these technological improvements was not to be reaped fully until after World War II. Elastic was first used in corsetry in 1911, but only for what were called "sports corsets," on which a strip of rubber about four inches long was sewn. In the 1930s these strips of rubber would be supplied by the Dunlop Company, better known today as a manufacturer of rubber tires.

During World War I, elastic supporting belts were made for women who worked at heavy labor. Other models were designed for women who worked in cabarets; in the United States these were called "dancing corsets."

However, elastic saw only very limited use during the 1920s, as rubber was crude and available only in short lengths. To give a garment elasticity, the rubber was sewn on in small strips, either flat or in gussets. In 1923, a rather unhygienic corset—and one that was difficult to put on—was cut from sheet rubber; it was known by the bizarre name of "Madame X." In 1930 the Charneau Company also introduced a corset made entirely of rubber, but it was perforated to let the skin breathe. Marginally more comfortable if just as hideous as its predecessor, this model stayed on the market until 1960.

The corset-makers of this period were actually stumbling in the dark, and the models they developed seem in retrospect particularly inept—despite being billed as the underwear of the modern woman. Manufacturers were baffled by a technical difficulty: latex, the sap of the hevea tree, hardened quickly and was therefore exported in bricks. Reconstituted rubber, made by adding various chemicals, was stretched into sheets and then cut into strips. But about 1930 it was finally discovered that latex could be kept liquid by being mixed with ammonia, and it began to be exported in barrels. Using the liquid latex, Dunlop developed a process for producing fine elastic yarn in any length imaginable. The latex was poured into glass capillary tubes, then passed through several acid baths before finally coagulating. This was Lastex, a yarn as fine as any made from traditional fibers.

Left, a Kestos corselet, illustrated by Brenot for *Vogue*, 1947. Below, an advertisement for the Bustidéal bra, *c.* 1920 (Bibliothèque des Arts Décoratifs, Paris).

Enfin ! Voilà l'Idéal...

105

Though cafés were still primarily a man's domain, three modern young ladies, right, sip lemonades at a café terrace in July 1929. Below, an elegant motorcyclist wearing a fur coat, around 1930. In order to straddle her fearsome engine, the lady must have abandoned wearing a corset.

At the same time, machines capable of weaving the new elastic yarns were developed, and these soon produced the first stretchy fabrics so essential to corsetry. The corset was no longer a rigid cage applied to a woman's body but a close-fitting and supportive garment, expanding as the body moved and breathed. Thanks to elasticized fabrics, there was no further need for hooks, laces, or tabs. A corset could now be slipped on, like the famous Roll-on, which grew so popular in the United States and Great Britain that the word "corset" fell into disuse; it was manufactured on a circular knitting machine like a sock.

New elasticized fabrics were now developed. A cambric and a muslin made of Lastex, for example, appeared on the market. Catalogues from the

thirties announced that "the best manufacturers use Lastex." Everywhere there was talk of this "miracle yarn."

Starting in 1930, makers of foundation garments tried to accommodate the varieties of the female form by offering better-fitting underwear and a greater range of sizes. The Gossard Company of the United States had paved the way early in the century by publishing a chart defining nine basic body types for women. In 1926, the Berlei Company of Australia commissioned two professors from the University of Sydney to conduct the first anthropometric study. Twenty-six measurements were taken of each of the five thousand women in the study. An analysis of the results showed that there existed five types of women. (The accuracy of this study was confirmed in Great Britain in 1976.) The Berlei stores offered a wide selection of sizes, and their sales staff performed alterations to en-

Her bonnet fringed with down and her silk satin slip split along the side to reveal baggy bloomers, the whole covered with lace panels, this British model minces for the camera in foundation garments typical of the 1920s—soft, light, fluid, and easy to slip on. Both attractive and comfortable, this underwear was in tune with the sports activities of the new woman: tennis, bicycling, parachuting, automobile racing. . . .

sure that the corsets fitted their clients well. Three to seven adjustments could be made on each corset. Yet despite these laudable efforts, women complained for a long time that "their corsets were killing them." Taking up the cry, Playtex would launch an advertising campaign thirty years later in which a lady grimaces and groans, "My girdle is killing me," followed by the delighted discovery of the "I Can't Believe It's a Girdle" girdle, the qualities of which are then touted.

In 1930, the bra became an established item of apparel in the United States. The key concept was widely seen to be the support a bra gave, and the advertisements from this period all stress the word "support."

In 1931, the Warner Company invented a fabric that was elastic in both directions, warp and woof, creating a small revolution. Later the company invented the fitted cup, sizes A to D, and the elastic strap. Warner's would also develop the seamless cup that was to have such great success in the 1970s. Many French manufacturers claim to have invented styles that for the most part came from the United States, such as the strapless bra or the backless bra that crosses behind at waist level.

Although the bra was now coming into general use, the corset was at its last spectacular gasp. One of the final innovations was the zippered corset. The first zipper closure had been patented by a Chicago engineer at the end of the nineteenth century, but it had the drawback of opening unexpectedly. In 1911, a Swede named Gideon Sundback developed a corset that could be removed in seconds. His invention did not reach stores until the 1930s, however, and as the fastenings were clumsy, the zippered corset flopped, despite the appeal of its concept.

In 1935 a padded cup was developed for women with small breasts. Three

With her devouring appetite for men, her triple-thick eyelashes, and her extravagant and revealing clothes, Mae West, left, made it her business to shock her puritan compatriots. Below, the effervescent Suzy Delair, wearing a skimpy outfit in the film *Lady Panama*, 1949.

years later underwired bras were introduced that made the breasts stick out. With the war imminent, these disappeared, only to resurface with a vengeance in the 1950s. A precursor of the fashion for imperious breasts was Mae West, who was at the height of her career in the 1920s and 1930s. She became the object of a veritable witch hunt when, in 1934, the censors' bureau of the American film industry prohibited studios from showing, among other things, women in underclothes, navels, breasts, scenes of adultery or childbirth, and bedrooms—unless they had twin beds. Kisses were timed with a stopwatch, necklines measured to a fraction of an inch. Mae West, with her spectacular chest, was a living insult to decency.

A Hitchcock mystery: in this
still photo taken on the set of
Psycho, Janet Leigh is wearing a
black bra—the famous wired
bra with circular stitching—yet
in the film itself her bra is
white. One theory is that the
change was made to avoid trig-
gering a hysterical reac-
tion from the Legion of
Decency, which would
have recoiled in hor-
ror at the sight of a
black lace bra.

In Europe, the great fashion designer Elsa Schiaparelli paid homage to Hollywood's queen of provocation in her own way. Her 1937 collection was named "Shocking," and she created a new perfume whose bottle was in the form of Mae West. "Schiap," who liked the idea that a woman should be free and brimful of fantasy, invented extravagant hats and jewelry but always kept to a feminine silhouette and advocated lightweight bras.

In the United States, it was only at the end of the war, with the release of *The Outlaw* and its revelation of Jane Russell's cleavage, that the Hollywood sex bomb again became a popular and licit figure in American culture.

One of the all-time best-sellers in the history of the bra appeared in 1939. It had deeper cups than usual and circular topstitching, which made for very shapely and very pointed breasts (sometimes the tip was even reinforced). This model, which reached the height of its glory in the 1950s, was brought back into fashion in the 1980s by Jean-Paul Gaultier, who would incorporate it humorously into his dress and bustier designs.

The American Du Pont Company began research in 1929 to make a new and stronger synthetic yarn, using phenol, hydrogen, and nitric acid. The research was carried out by Dr. Wallace H. Carrothers and his team. In October 1938, Du Pont publicly announced the discovery of nylon. At the New York World's Fair the following year it exhibited the first nylon stockings. Two years later the first complete set of nylon undergarments was introduced. With the United States's entry into the war, however, nylon could no longer be used for lingerie. Available reserves were mobilized for the war effort to make tents, rope, and military tarpaulins.

The war brought with it a host of restrictions, and women responded with characteristic ingenuity. When stockings became unavailable they used leg makeup and penciled in the seam with an eyebrow pencil; for day wear they cut patterns out of upholstery fabric. In the corset industry, steel stays were rationed, and rubber imports were also affected. Nylon, which had gone to make parachutes during the war, was used again to make bras afterward, with little shift in the basic geometry. The new fabric was phenomenally successful: it was light, shiny, wear-resistant, quick-drying, and wrinkle-free. It had everything needed to capture the lingerie sector. After the Stone Age and the Iron Age came the Age of Nylon. Fine lingerie was no longer the prerogative of a privileged social class, and its universal availability signaled a trend that was to spread through fashion generally.

In 1940 Hollywood's embodiment of the ideal woman was no longer Mae West but Katharine Hepburn. She was young, emancipated, and sporty looking, and wore pants, a pullover, and flat shoes. The liberating influence of ready-to-wear clothing—it was practical, comfortable, healthy, and cheap—spread across the world from the United States. The vogue for pullovers and

Katharine Hepburn brought into vogue a different kind of sophistication: soft hairstyle, light make-up, and a liberated attitude.

Overleaf, a few light moments relating to the bra in film. Top row, left to right, Simone Signoret, Robert Mitchum, and Woody Allen. Bottom row, Charlie Chaplin, Marcello Mastroianni, and Sophia Loren.

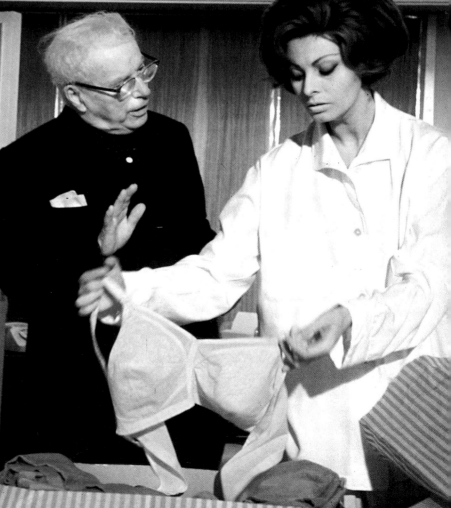

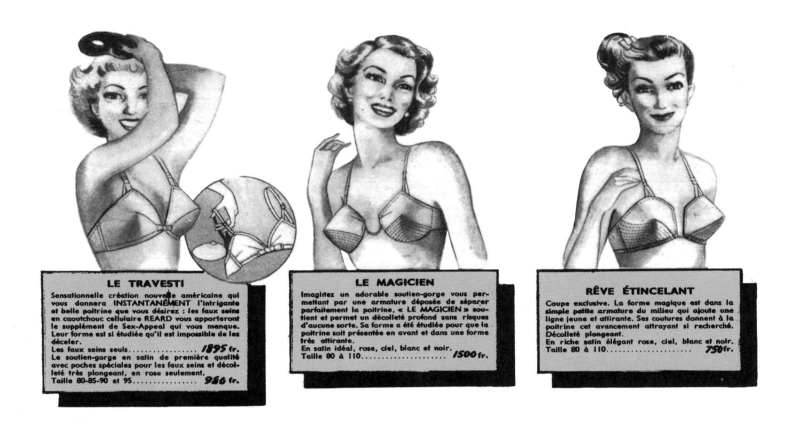

LE TRAVESTI

Sensationnelle création nouvelle américaine qui vous donnera INSTANTANÉMENT l'intrigante et belle poitrine que vous désirez : les faux seins en caoutchouc cellulaire RÉARD vous apporteront le supplément de Sex-Appeal qui vous manque. Leur forme est si étudiée qu'il est impossible de les déceler.
Les faux seins seuls.................. *1895* fr.
Le soutien-gorge en satin de première qualité avec poches spéciales pour les faux seins et décolleté très plongeant, en rose seulement.
Taille 80-85-90 et 95................ *986* fr.

LE MAGICIEN

Imaginez un adorable soutien-gorge vous permettant par une armature déposée de séparer parfaitement la poitrine, « LE MAGICIEN » soutient et permet un décolleté profond sans risques d'aucune sorte. Sa forme a été étudiée pour que la poitrine soit présentée en avant et dans une forme très attirante.
En satin idéal, rose, ciel, blanc et noir.
Taille 80 à 110.................... *1500* fr.

RÊVE ÉTINCELANT

Coupe exclusive. La forme magique est dans la simple petite armature du milieu qui ajoute une ligne jeune et attirante. Ses coutures donnent à la poitrine cet avancement attrayant si recherché. Décolleté plongeant.
En riche satin élégant rose, ciel, blanc et noir.
Taille 80 à 110..................... *750* fr.

"Réard, the bra of the stars, will make stars of your breasts!" read the appalling slogan of the French company that first marketed the bikini. The names of its designs—Divine Love, which "invites romance on a wisp of cigarette smoke"; Little Sorcerer; Ardent Desire—outdid each other in suaveness. The advertisement concluded, "All these bras are worn by the greatest American film stars! Thanks to Réard, they are now offered to you." Opposite right, the first string bikini, introduced on July 5, 1946, at a pool in Paris, where it provoked a furor on the part of the public. Opposite left, the black lace *guêpière* by Star, 1956 (Bibliothèque Forney, Paris).

tight-fitting sweaters also came from the United States. The bra contributed to a complete reworking of the silhouette: the breasts were higher.

After the war, European women found themselves fascinated by the lifestyle of their American counterparts, with their nylon stockings, their chewing gum, their swing, and their mild tobacco. But the relaxed style of Americans sometimes hid a terrible puritanism. When the first bathing-beauty contest took place in Paris in 1946, the correspondents of the *Herald Tribune* were shocked, especially by an item created by the Réard Company—the bikini, a tiny two-piece bathing suit that used the strict legal minimum of fabric. A long hibernation awaited the bikini, and it would only reemerge in the 1960s when the Beach Boys look splashed across the United States.

Often the fads that surface after a war have their roots in prewar fashions. Quiescent while the battle rages, they recover their vividness in peacetime.

Tellingly, 1940 was the year when the shaped silhouette first reappeared. "All you need," said *Vogue*, "is to have a waist, maintained if necessary by a light corset." The trend disappeared during the war, but returned in 1947 with Christian Dior's New Look. A short period of euphoria followed, when luxury and the female form were exalted. The style offered an image of women as flowers—elegant, the bust well defined, the waist prettily cinched. Skirts grew longer, while the short corset and Marcel Rochas's *guêpière* came into vogue.

BREASTS LIKE MISSILE SILOS

It has been remarked that "Women are the only mammals whose mammary globes are always visible, both to their own eyes and to those of others." In 1950, the trend was more than ever toward globe-shaped breasts, carried high. The pin-up aesthetic was going full tilt: Jane Russell, Gina Lollobrigida, Jayne Mansfield, Sophia Loren, and Anita Ekberg swirled through men's fantasies.

The infatuation with big breasts, writes F. Henriquez, "can be explained only if we attribute to the overgenerous bosom of Miss Mansfield the consoling power of the maternal breast, which each man misses to a greater or lesser extent." One of the psychoanalytic theories that is advanced to explain the vogue for billowy breasts is that in the famished world that followed the war years—just as in the years that followed the Napoleonic era—the hypertrophied female breast functioned as a sort of nourishing and consoling pillow.

Bosoms and bras played starring roles in films the world over. In the films of Russ Meyer and Federico Fellini, women often have breasts of astounding size, which are actually proportional to the breast as seen by a nursing infant. Yet one of Russ Meyer's films, *Mamell's Story*, belies this analysis somewhat,

The new leading ladies, with their fascinating bosoms: above, Mamie Van Doren; opposite, clockwise from top left, Gina Lollobrigida, Jane Russell, Jayne Mansfield, and Marilyn Monroe.

117

Jane Russell, of the hyperbolic bust, in her first film, *The Outlaw*, 1943, a western directed by Howard Hughes. Russell was to conduct her career with great brio, acting for the greatest filmmakers of her time, from Howard Hawks to Raoul Walsh, by way of Nicholas Ray and John Sturges.

Opposite, the famous "net" by Lou, this one the Paprika.

since Chesty Morgan (bust seventy-nine inches) plays a dangerous criminal who suffocates her victims between her breasts.

The film producer and airplane designer Howard Hughes set his talents to inventing an aerodynamic bra reinforced with wiring, a veritable shelf, the only thing that could support the breasts of Jane Russell, who played the female lead in his film *The Outlaw*. At the start of shooting, her bras either squashed her breasts or else provided insufficient support, so that they visibly bounced. When Hughes took issue, the costume mistress declared that she was a designer, not an architect. The film was not released until five years after its completion, thanks to the powerful lobbying of the American Legion of Decency. Yet the male lead seems to have been mainly intent on relating to his horse, despite Jane Russell's thirty-eight-inch bust.

In Blake Edwards's *Operation Petticoat*, Tony Curtis commands a submarine that is being pursued by the Japanese. He orders his female crew to help pretend the submarine has sunk by using the time-honored strategy of propelling various objects and equipment out the torpedo launch-tubes. But instead of the usual life jackets and oil drums, dozens of bras bob up to the ocean's surface.

LOU *jeune France*

Women managed to give themselves breasts like nuclear warheads thanks to the famous bra with circular top-stitching invented in 1939. In France, Mme Fallère, the designer for the Lou Company, launched an "American-style" model. Working in the small town of Nancy with two sewing machines, she began her career because she had a larger-than-normal bosom and could never find a bra to fit her. Lou bras gained a reputation for cupping the breasts nicely and giving a shapely curve to the bust. In the 1970s, Mme Fallère commissioned a special lace that she used in designing an enormously successful bra—the *filet de Lou*, or Lou "net." The lace truly does resemble netting, as though the breasts were imprisoned behind fine mesh. The bra came in white, camel, and caramel and gave the breasts a pretty, rounded form, its only inconvenience being that it cut into the nipple and, when one took it off, left a mesh imprint on the tips of the breasts. But women liked the Lou "nets." Mme Fallère, a colorful character in corsetry, is also the inventor of the scientific method of putting on a bra. The trick is to bend over at right angles so that one's breasts

Paprika
Paprika
Paprika

le nouveau coloris
de LOU

c'est jeune, c'est gai,
c'est pétillant et dynamique

filet
de LOU

Soutien-gorge   35 F
Slip   22 F

A visit to the corset shop, at the beginning of the 1950s. The lady in the hat can choose from a number of items with enticing names: Pink Champagne, Merry Widow, or the somewhat more chic Charade, Renoir, or Camellia. The undergarment she is admiring in the photograph, a slip with a very lightly boned corselet, was one of the more popular at the time.

hang down vertically, slip on the bra, and fasten it by contorting one's arms. It may be the best method, but it takes the agility of a yogi to perform!

In 1951 Warner's came out with a new item of lingerie, an elasticized satin girdle joined to a wired bra, called a Merry Widow (after Franz Liszt's operetta), which was particularly appreciated for evening wear. In 1952 a nylon bra, the Very Secret, was introduced for women with undersized breasts; it had extremely thin air cushions that could be blown up at will. During the same period, Trois Suisses, the French mail-order company, published a catalogue that was entirely devoted to lingerie. The New Look of the postwar years had brought back the vogue for frilly foundation garments, and the best part was that they no longer needed to be ironed, thanks to their nylon construction. Fine lingerie began to appear. In 1955, new models made of black nylon lace were introduced. A year later the push-up bra, an American invention, was developed by France's Lejaby. The push-up bra achieved its effect by having the straps attach to the ends of the wiring, practically at the armpits. The cut of the bra brought the breasts together, and the wiring and straps lifted them up.

"Plush is a sort of deep-piled velvet. It is narrow. It serves as a buffer between a stay, laces or a fastener and the point of contact with the skin," reads a passage from a 1958 opus on corsets, girdles, and bras. What supplies were needed to make a bra during the 1950s? The answers can all be found in this book, coyly signed "Mademoiselle Etienne." The preface was written by Marie-Rose Lebigot, the woman who designed France's first strapless demi-cup bra. The foreword announces that the manual is intended to provide for students of technical colleges and vocational centers—and also for "women who

Carol Baker, below, the former nightclub dancer who played the sexy ingenue in *Baby Doll*, 1958, reclining in a black lace bra and panties.

are clever with their hands"—"useful advice in making their own handiwork. . . . The knowledge of a few procedures will allow them to tailor their own bras. Finally, I would like to help female apprentices who, for family or social reasons, sometimes very painful ones, have entered the work force directly at the age of fourteen. They come to our schools once a week to attend required professional courses. And if some of the girls are there only because they are obliged to and it allows their family to receive additional welfare payments, the dedication with which others apply themselves to acquiring the beauty of texts as well as the beauty of forms is moving to behold. We pray with all our heart that this little book will help them to understand their trade intelligently and further master it." This passage tells a great deal about the presiding moral order and the conditions of employment among dressmaker's apprentices.

Setting aside these maternalistic comments, the book offers detailed information on all the elements that go into making a bra. The frames, wires, and dividers are small stainless metal bars fashioned according to their various uses. Some are placed below the breasts, while others are attached to the upper edge of the bra or bustier. There are also V-shaped dividers that are smaller than the frames; these go in front, to allow a deeper décolletage.

In 1958, with the sexual revolution only a few years off, some of the customs inherited from the nineteenth century still survived. Despite the fact that most women now wore girdles, there were still corsets being worn—and not simply by a few elderly ladies, since Mademoiselle Etienne's handbook contains instructions for making children's corsets. These replaced and complemented the Velpeau strip, which "supports and protects the stomach, preventing it from reaching an exaggerated size as in some

Examples of corselets, bras, panties, and girdles by France's Aubade company, displayed by models in affected poses.

LA SANA BÉBÉ
LA SANETTE
soutien idéal
de l'abdomen
Fabrique : 61, rue Saint-Charles — PARIS

Advertisement for a corset for young girls, above. Until the middle of the twentieth century, it was believed that a child's body had to be molded. Right, Jayne Mansfield disembarking from a plane at the London airport, surrounded by a crowd of photographers.

children," according to the author, who goes on to give all the information necessary to make corsets for wearers of all ages. "Their purpose is to support the spine and the shoulder blades, as a garden stake supports the stem of a plant." Oddly enough, it is only girls who must wear them, starting from the age of four, whereas little boys are thought to not need them.

At the dawn of the rock and roll era, Mademoiselle Etienne was drawing up a catalogue of the many kinds of stiffening bones available to the corset-maker. Whalebone strips, made from the baleen of whales, were still in use in the late 1950s. They even belonged to two categories: those from whales caught in the South Seas and Antarctic waters, and those (of inferior quality) from the Atlantic sperm whale. Baleen consists of the elastic, horny plates that grow on the upper jaw of certain whales in thin parallel strips like the pages of a book. On the average, a whale carries 250 to 300 plates of baleen, each up to three or four yards long, and together weighing 3,500 pounds. Once removed

agent secret
de votre charme
STAR
DÉVOILE SON DERNIER MODÈLE
"Caresses" bustier ou soutien-gorge
en taffetas nylon garni de dentelle

Conçu pour vous avantager
IL VALORISE "EN TOUTE DISCRÉTION"
Étudié pour se faire oublier
IL SOUTIENT "EN TOUT CONFORT"
Seul à posséder une telle classe-couture
IL VOUS SERT "EN TOUTE ÉLÉGANCE"

Borrowing its ambience from film noir, this advertisement—a fairly original one by the vapid and conformist standards of the period—promotes the Caresse bra, from Star.

from the whale, the baleen is cleaned and cut along the grain into sections according to thickness, then further reduced to long narrow strips or "bones" of varying width. To make sawing easier, the whalebone is first softened in warm water. Finally it is sanded and polished, cut to lengths, and rounded on the ends. The bone is slid into the corset so that the smooth side will face toward the woman's body. "Boning" also refers to the steel strips covered with paper, fabric, or leather that are used in corsetry. Boning was also made from turkey feathers and, finally, from nylon and other plastics, which eventually replaced all other materials.

FOUNDATION GARMENTS FOR THE YOUNG MISS

In the early 1960s in the United States and Great Britain, the corsetry industry began to take notice of a new group of buyers—teenage girls. In less than twenty years, household incomes had more than tripled, and parents could now afford to give their children pocket money. A whole generation awoke to the joys of consumerism—45-rpm records, cosmetics, ballet slippers, and bras. And a new kind of underwear was introduced that was softer and simpler.

The print panties, demi-cup bra, and loosely piled hair of the 1960s teenager announced a new and carefree generation. Above, a bra and girdle by Aubade. Opposite, an American design.

These new models were to have an important consequence for the future, since all the little girls who grew up wearing entirely comfortable panties and bras would later demand the same in adult women's undergarments. The trends that surfaced first in teenage designs would in any case influence all of lingerie. For millions of women, daily life was becoming simpler and more practical. In 1960, a basic design improvement made life easier: bras were finally equipped with adjustable elastic straps. Before, the straps were kept from sliding down onto the arms by a small strip of fabric attached by a snap to the inside of the garment.

It was also in 1960 that one of the most important inventions of the century was introduced—namely, the first oral contraceptive, developed by the American Gregory Pincus. This was to have unexpected repercussions in the field of lingerie, since the bust measurements of young girls would increase almost an inch over the next two decades, a windfall for bra manufacturers.

The bra enclosed the breasts, while the girdle and panties were high and reinforced—dreaded items, apparently, among adolescent boys. These undergarments from the Warner line were featured in a 1965 issue of *Marie-Claire*, photographs by J.-J. Bugat.

As the lingerie market became more and more lucrative, it instigated unusually innovative advertising campaigns. In 1963, a campaign put the bra manufacturer Rosy in the news. The photograph, taken by Jean-Loup Sieff, shows a woman covering her breasts with her arms and holding a rose in her hand—the product never even appears in the ad. In 1964 on the beaches of Saint-Tropez, a number of women were less reticent about revealing their breasts—the monokini had arrived.

Also in the 1960s, the Playtex Company opened up new paths with its distribution system. It would become the resident heavyweight and over-

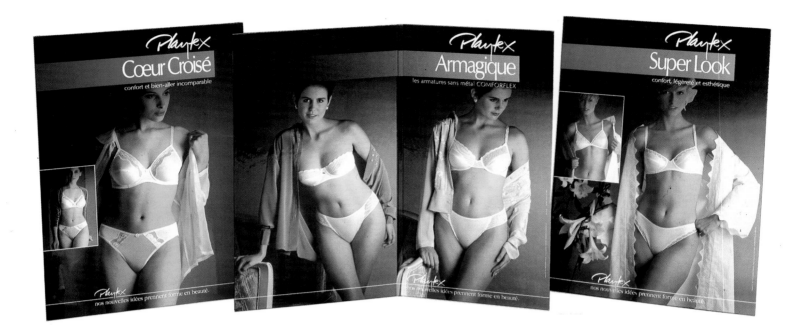

Playtex was founded in 1932 by an American chemist whose first product, made entirely of latex, was a bathing cap. Gradually, his product line expanded to include bras and girdles, but it took more than thirty years for his undergarments to become international best-sellers: in 1969, the Cross Your Heart bra; in 1971, the 18-hour Girdle; in 1973, the I Can't Believe It's a Girdle girdle; in 1985 the Armagique bra.

whelming market leader. The company had been started in the United States in 1932 by a Mr. Spanel, an art amateur with a particular fascination for Gothic cathedrals. The first products designed by the company were rather hideous all-rubber girdles, which were sold rolled up in metal tubes. But it was after World War II, with the invention of spanette, a new elastic yarn named after the founder, that the Playtex Company really took off. Spanette, which had been developed in the Playtex research laboratories in Paramus, New Jersey, was used to make the "Eighteen-hour Girdle," a girdle that could be worn for a long period without becoming uncomfortable.

In the early 1950s, Playtex addressed itself to the problem of the bra. The company rarely introduced a product unless it had patented it first, for there

was—and still is—almost always something exclusive about a Playtex design. The famous "Cross Your Heart" bra, for instance, had the frame in a cross pattern. The "I Can't Believe It's a Girdle" girdle, far and away the market leader, provides enormous support while weighing just over two ounces. A new model bra contains plastic wiring and no metal. It took three years of research to develop the wiring, which is always a source of great technical difficulty for the bra manufacturer. The wiring must not pierce the bra during machine-washing, it must not lose its shape or break, and it must be pliable and comfortable for the wearer. The development of the new system was all the more important as the trend toward wired bras has increased, particularly in the last few years. Market share was for a long time at around 35 percent, but has risen to 55 percent since 1990. Women between twenty-five and forty now prefer bras that push up their breasts, just as their mothers did in the 1950s.

But the all-time leader on the brassiere hit parade is still the Cross Your Heart bra, model 556, whose name resonates in everyone's memory. Today it has something of an old-fashioned image, which Playtex is trying to combat, since the company has a special affection for it. This "historic" bra, introduced nearly thirty years ago, is still selling 800,000 units a year in France alone, and earning the company fifteen million dollars in sales. With a single model, one that is classic and not particularly sexy, Playtex is able to match the total gross sales for the fifteenth-largest lingerie producer in France.

Sociologists observed in the 1960s that the more developed a society becomes and the more its population is able to eat to satiety, the more its women are required to be thin. Undernourished societies, by contrast, admire well-padded women. At the height of the 1960s the most fashionable figures were flat-as-a-board Englishwomen with big fake eyelashes, like Jane Birkin or the quasi-skeletal Twiggy.

In 1968, the Miss America pageant set off a conflagration. Feminists were throwing away their bras and setting fire to them. The Marine Guard at the

In the 1990s Playtex launched a campaign to reinvent its image along more modern and youthful lines. Its bras became lighter and more revealing, with embroidery and scalloping, and thong panties are now to be found among its line of girdles and quasi-orthopedic bras.

doors to the Senate in Washington, D.C., looked on impassively at the surreal bonfire and at the militant Women's Libbers yelling and singing. The emancipation of the breast was at hand. Bare nipples resided under form-fitting sweaters and Indian tunics. The titillating game at the time was to determine whether a girl was wearing a bra or not. Women had several motivations for abandoning the bra: one was obviously to make women free of all constraints, and the bra was the last constraining element of female dress; but another was to set themselves off from preceding generations. Young women were asserting their youth and rebelling against their middle-class mothers, who were stuck because their anatomy made it much more difficult for them to give up the bra, compared to their twenty-year-old daughters.

In France there was one firm that became narrowly identified with the new generation, the Dimanche Company, which in 1962 introduced the first seamless bra. In 1965 it shortened its name, and Dim was born. In 1968 the company became famous for its tights, marketed in a little cardboard box for a dollar a pair. One-quarter the price of a classic pair of stockings, these tights were all the more indispensable as the miniskirt had swept every town, relegating the garter belt so idolized by men to the back shelf. During the tights years, fashion belonged to women with small breasts and long legs, who walked in giant strides and delighted in new attitudes. In 1975 Dim decided to create its own line of lingerie.

In 1970 Dim had already taken the step of releasing a sort of bra that was manufactured in the Dim tights factories. It was knit, the cups were made from heel sections, and the parts were joined by the same elastic bands used for panties. This gossamer dressing for the breasts was sold in every color, rolled into a ball in a small box, with matching panties available. Cheerful and cheap, the bra-and-panty sets caught the spirit of the times. But while these saucy creations did interpret a widely held desire to feel young and rebellious, they made no attempt to hold up the breasts.

SOUTIEN-GORGE FLEUR DE DENTELLE

DIM

Dim
moi tout

Generous busts came back into fashion in the 1980s. During that decade, a number of products unrelated to lingerie were promoted by models with large, milk-white bosoms.

Dim knew its products were novelty items. Running a lingerie company is no easy matter when you are a tights manufacturer. At first, the company paid for its inexperience by projecting the wrong image. Its ads borrowed from what had worked with tights and showed clips of women actively jumping around. Lingerie campaigns needed to be more intimate—and more credible. Hopping around made women's breasts bounce, Dim soon realized, and the effect was disastrous. By choosing a large-bosomed model named Rosemary to represent the company, Dim consciously created a different image for itself. Today the firm stresses its supportive bras for generous busts, frilly on top and solid below.

One of the first molded cups had been patented before World War II. The advent of polyester and nylon made it possible to manufacture panties and molded bras at high temperatures, using tools inspired by the new automotive and aerospace industries. Warner's introduced a bra with a seamless molded cup, called the Special Pull. Wearing it, a woman gave the impression of having bare breasts.

It was the particularly innovative Huit Company that, in 1970, introduced the first molded bra in France. Huit targeted teenagers and women who chose the natural look, offering bras made of voile or tulle that were as light and supple as air. The product was new, as was its marketing. In one of the first instances of novelty packaging, the bra was coiled inside a plastic bubble, and the item sold in supermarkets. Huit also created the first ad campaigns to run in movie houses. They show a young mermaid diving into the water and climbing out onto a rock—the message is of freshness, naturalness, and freedom. Needless to say, Huit quickly carved itself a successful position. All the ads for Huit showed a woman gamboling against a background of unspoiled nature or ocean. Never provocative, and even somewhat prudish and sentimental, these campaigns offered a counterpoint to what the other manufacturers were doing. A little later, Huit introduced coordinates (the little bubble now had two compartments), then a bra that was both seamless and unsewn. It was welded and stitched together by ultrasound (1973). One of Huit's leading styles was the

The Quito bra by Huit, above, which "you slip on like a vest and close in front," made of Terylene crêpe jersey. Left, another bra by Huit, perhaps the most transparent one ever made.

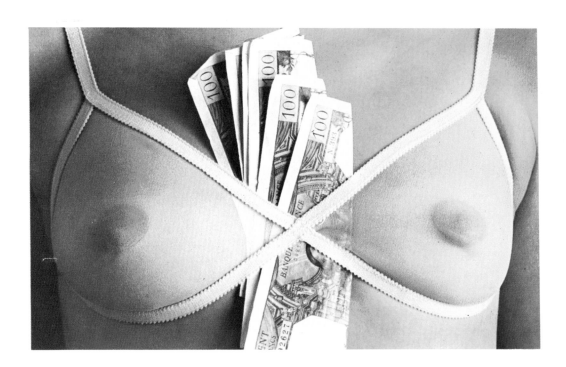

Two best-sellers belonging to different decades. From the 1970s, the Titcha by Huit, above, with "an elastic band under the cups that keeps the bra from riding up." In fact, it often needed to be readjusted. Lou's Rio bra from the late 1980s, opposite, sold out in a few weeks.

Titcha, which sold five million units for six years running. Huit was also the first manufacturer to offer a reasonably priced silk bra, just as it was among the first to sign on to the trend for all-cotton underwear.

Yet despite its creative spirit, the company suffered a cropper in the molded-bra market, steadfastly believing it would take off in the late 1970s and 1980s. In fact, molded bras have remained a fairly narrow market. And when the natural look fell flat in the mid-1970s, Huit began to experience financial difficulties, which were aggravated by the oil crisis. The company filed for bankruptcy in 1978, then resumed operations, only to go belly-up again two years later. Women's outlooks had changed, and Huit's products were no longer in step with the consumer. Everything that had made the company a success was now a liability. Women found its bras soft, unsupportive, too transparent—in a word, insubstantial. The last buyer to take over the company changed its direction radically, introducing a more modern and more feminine line, with a selection of printed cotton products.

The fashion for going braless would result in many lingerie manufacturers going out of business. At first France was far and away the foremost bra producer in the world, with more than two hundred manufacturers in the late 1960s; today there are hardly fifteen. Yet, by an irony of fate, the student uprisings and other events that brought freer social mores and the pill also made women's breasts increase in size. Fifteen years ago the average bust measurement in France was about thirty-three inches; today it is thirty-five inches—thirty-seven inches among younger women. So if the sexual revolution brought financial ruin to a number of manufacturers, in the long run it aided those who survived or were late entrants to the market. Having larger breasts in most cases means having to wear a good bra.

In the 1950s, researchers developed resins that could be blended with almost any fabric: cotton, linen, rayon, silk, nylon, even tulle and lace. In 1950, the Du Pont Company—always a leader—invented Lycra, an extremely stretchy knit made of two yarns, one synthetic (polyester or polyamide), accounting for 85 percent, and the other a very light elastic

Illustrations by Moebius for Lili Cube stretch garments, which fit into small cardboard boxes. Items such as the bra-dress, below, exploit the shape of the bust with great humor.

fiber (spandex), accounting for 15 percent. But it would take more than thirty years for the researchers to develop the ideal fabric. A number of serious technical problems had to be resolved first: dyeing the polyesters at extremely high temperatures destroyed the spandex, swimming pool chlorine damaged the fibers, and white spots appeared on the polyamide as soon as its stitches were stretched.

When the new textile finally exploded onto the market in the 1980s, it spelled the end for clips, yokes, zippers, and fasteners. Lycra, a magic fiber, could be invisibly incorporated into the finest and most fluid materials, including silk, crepe, tulle, and lace. A natural or synthetic fiber blended with 2 to 4 percent Lycra will make a garment that will cling to every curve of the body. The fiber can be stretched to four or five times its own length and recover instantly. Fine, soft, and ultra-stretchy, it feels like a second skin, arousing totally new sensations in the women wearing it. Here finally was the dream fabric for making underwear.

By the late 1980s Lycra, with its perfect ability to sculpt the body, had penetrated to every recess of the fashion world, from the collections to ready-to-wear. As the designer Angelo Tarlazzi would say, "A stretch jersey dress is the antithesis of grannyhood!" Thanks to the technicians of today's textile industry, who are the modern alchemists of texture, it is even possible to make stretch muslin and stretch broderie anglaise, which the company Anti Flirt has used for matching bustiers and briefs.

An ultra-clingy outfit by Chantal Thomass, designed to be worn without a bra. For anyone who nonetheless needs support, mail-order catalogues and lingerie shops now offer sticky strips of plastic that lift the breasts. Below left, the item in question, available in a range of colors and with lace designs. Although claimed to be hypoallergenic and risk-free, some bras that glue to the underside of the breasts can tear off skin when they are removed.

139

THE BIG BANG OF LARGE CUPS

The wheel of history continually revolves, and in the 1980s there was a return to the rounded breast and the well-padded bosom. Wired bras increased their sales over all others. The high priestess of breasts ensconced in lacy demi-cups was the designer Chantal Thomass, and the entire profession has recognized her role in championing the turnaround.

If plague, famine, war, and exile fanned the collective penchant for the sheltering bosom in centuries past, what reason can our modern society have had, twenty years before the end of the millennium, for once again preferring proud breasts? Some suggest that the great economic crises of the 1970s were a contributing factor, while others point out that the trend really started in the early 1980s. At the start of the decade, 54 percent of women said they had never worn fine lingerie, according to a survey. Yet in 1983 that sector of the market boomed, in concert with stock-market profits.

Designers inspired by a new generation of textiles created a virtual explosion in lingerie. Bras came in only a few different types—no more than five basic constructions—but the consumer faced a dizzying array of styles on the lingerie shelves of department stores. Colors, prints, and textures were suddenly available in vast numbers, and in infinite combinations.

Twenty years before the end of the millennium, breasts were again magnified—somewhat in the style of Crete—dramatized, made prominent, shaped, and otherwise turned into a major decorative element of the female silhouette. Opposite, a design by Chantal Thomass, in which the bodice is trimmed with down. Above, a bra created by Italy's Samuel Mazza shortly before the dissolution of the USSR, and exhibited in a Milan gallery in May 1991.

Cherries, forget-me-nots, Provençal patterns—the underwear styles of Princesse Tam-Tam were surprising and captivating. The company was a pioneer in the field of printed bras, which saw considerable growth afterward. Opposite page, lacing from Thierry Mugler's 1991 summer collection (above left and below right) and two designs from the 1991 winter collection by Chantal Thomass (above right and below left).

In 1984, two sisters from Madagascar, Loumia and Shama Hiridjee, arrived in Paris and opened a novelty store. Men's gag underwear sold so briskly that they decided to invent an equivalent for women. A year later they opened a boutique in Paris with the percussive name of Princesse Tam-Tam. The two young designers would inspire considerable jealousy on the part of the big names in the business. They introduced a variety of bras: tartans, polka dots, cotton piqués with a raspberry or cherry motif, or with little bows between the breasts or rickrack along the top, and also braid-trimmed velvet bustiers and cotton or flannel pajamas, since the popularity of cocooning had led to a soft style of lingerie intended for home wear. For several years, women's magazines have been showing young women in cotton underwear, their hair tousled and their socks falling down around their ankles. As the

marketing directors put it in their inimitable jargon, it is "the era of the multi-faceted woman," a bedraggled wild woman in the morning and a femme fatale at night.

Thanks to the textile revolution, to Lycra, to the microfibers that give fabrics a peach-skin feel (the fibers are becoming finer and finer), to elasticized lace, and to stretch cotton in every print imaginable, from the African boubou to the traditional patterns of Provence, bras have attained an unprecedented level of refinement and comfort. In the ultrasophisticated category, one brand from Italy has come to be perceived as the Rolls-Royce of bras and panties: La Perla.

And as the history of fashion never stops reprising itself, the boned *guêpière* that draws in the waist is back in style. Poupie Cadolle, who provides corsets for the dancers at the Crazy Horse cabaret in Paris, is a fanatic partisan of this return to the past. She sighs for the waistlines of yesteryear. At the Crazy Horse, the very slimmest dancers measure twenty-three inches at the waist. "The average waistline today is twenty-five or twenty-five and a half inches. But the clients for our *guêpière* back in the 1950s had twenty-one-inch waists, like Brigitte Bardot and Martine Carol." But Cadolle readily admits that all is not lost. As an example, she cites certain young actresses from the Comédie-Française who came dragging their feet when they needed to be fitted for a corset. "Then when they try it on, their waist pinched in, their back supported, they feel it gives them the carriage of a queen." Japanese women, whose busts have also grown two sizes in the last ten years because of the pill and changes in diet, have corsets made for them primarily to mark their waists, which according to Poupie Cadolle are not naturally well defined.

Still on the subject of the exponential increase in the number of bras available, the great wave of shiny stretch fabrics that has flooded the world of lingerie and of fashion generally is of notable interest. It is as though it were now inconceivable to make clothes that do not stretch to the rhythm of our movements and our breathing. This is the influence of the fitness trend, which dates back to the mid-1970s. In the United States, Jane Fonda popularized aerobics with her series of videocassettes. In France, Véronique and Davina hosted a television program of gymnastics set to music. Lingerie benefited from the new sports and dance outfits—shorts and tights of shimmery stretch fabrics in a variety of

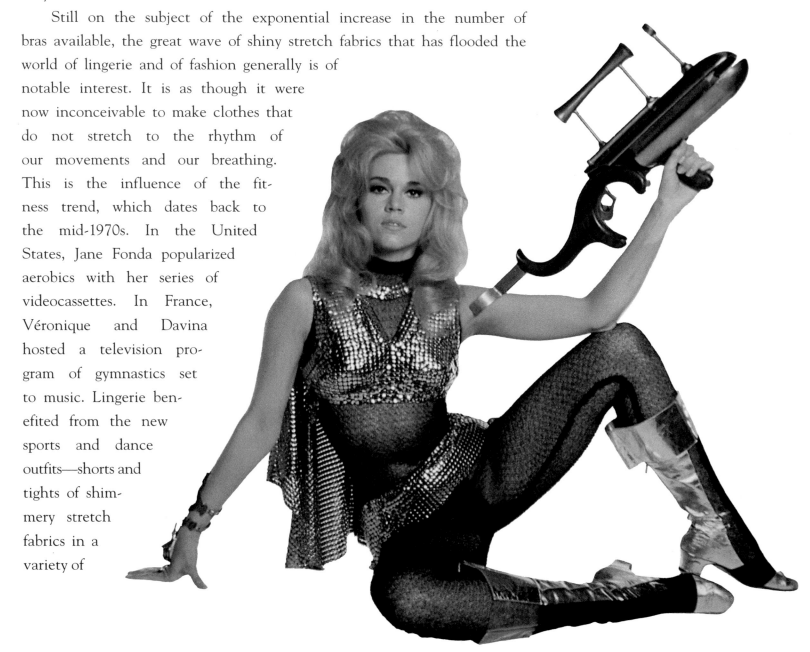

Jane Fonda, one of the great champions of body-sculpting through aerobics, showed off her Barbie-doll figure in 1968 in the title role of *Barbarella*, for which she wore in turn a Plexiglas and a metallic bra, below. Opposite, a *guêpière* by Warner.

Made of quilted pink satin, this cone-breasted *guêpière* by Jean-Paul Gaultier was worn by Madonna on her 1990 European tour. Thierry Mugler creations, opposite, clockwise from above left: "Diver," 1990 summer collection; "Built Like a Buick," winter 1989; "Shadow Show," summer 1991; and "Imanoid," summer 1991.

new colors. By an association of ideas, this kind of stretchy garment is identified with well-built women.

The obsession with slimming and the frantic energy poured into sculpting the body through weight training—isn't this a resurgence of the corset in another form? Our great-grandmothers were fully as preoccupied with maintaining the body, but used a boned straitjacket rather than muscles of steel and over-the-counter appetite suppressants. The latest incarnation of the bra is as bold innerwear-outerwear. Bodices, bustiers, and brassieres are being worn as items of apparel in their own right. The era of the outerwear bra was first popularized by Madonna and by the Eurhythmics' singer Annie Lennox, who

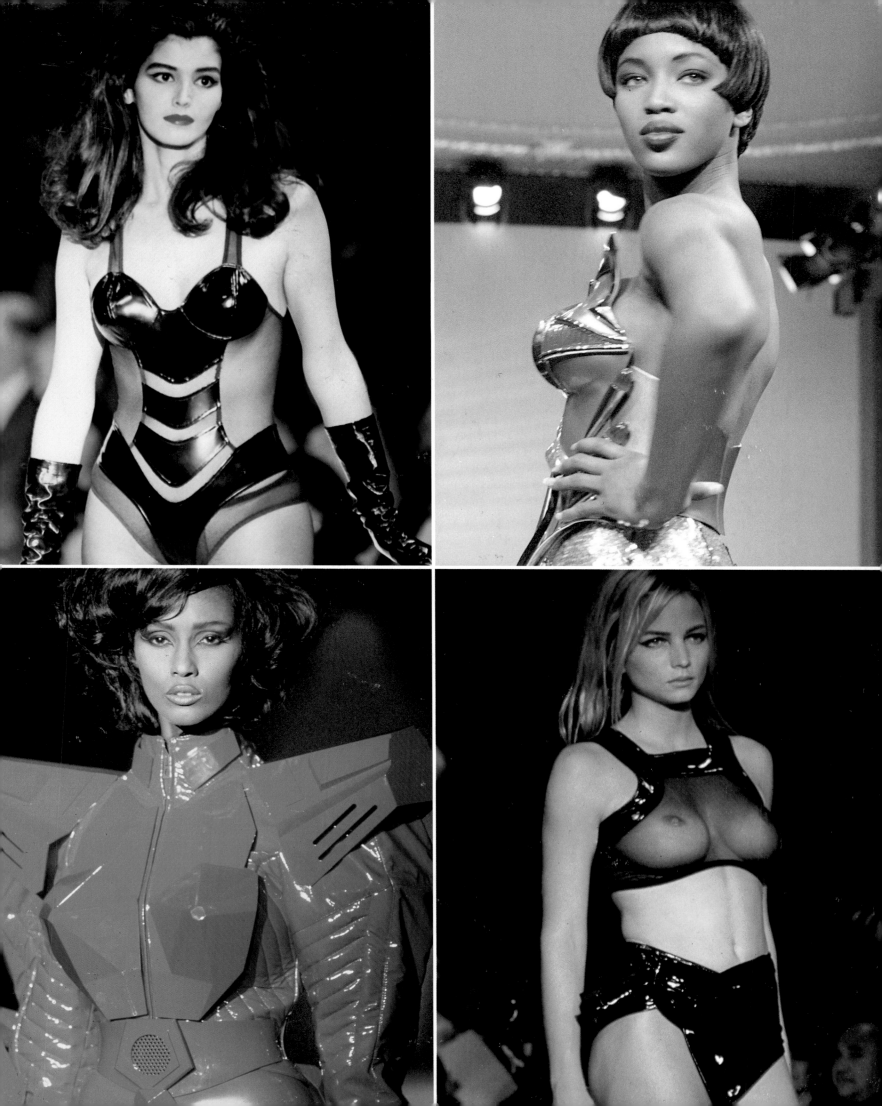

Above, a bra by Chantal Thomass, with little gathered flounces, 1991. Opposite, in the shade of a wide-brimmed rooster-feather confection, a La Perla bra (1992). Lace, pleated voile cups, tulle straps—the designs of this Italian maker are like a cunning and refined architecture.

appeared onstage in leather pants and a red lace bra. In 1988, Huit introduced the first velvet bra—unprecedented in lingerie—or more exactly a panne bra in bronze green, purple, or saffron. Though no one believed in these items, particularly the retailers, they sold briskly.

When a bra is seen hanging on a clothesline drying, it looks flimsy and comical, but in fact it is a high-precision industrial product. To make one takes twenty or more pieces, in tulle, jersey, or lace—some of them tiny. The first stage is the creation of an incredible puzzle, designed by the pattern-makers, so that when cutting the miles of fabric that pass through the work-shop little waste will be left over. Then comes the assembly, which for a moderately sophisticated style may require thirty separate steps, performed by thirty different workers. Stitching, accurate to within a millimeter, fastening off, whipstitching—each operator has only a few seconds to perform her piece-meal task.

The bra is the most complex item of dress there is and cannot be made by a machine. Corsetry, in consequence, remains a labor-intensive trade. As has happened in many other areas of the textile industry, its manufacturers have gone abroad to build their factories—to Portugal, Tunisia, Morocco, Greece, and Turkey.

All the steps prior to assembly have been computerized and mechanized. But the moment it comes to actually constructing the bra, the best that can be done is to separate the different operations. Each worker—and they are generally women—is charged with a single stitch, perhaps a very small one. Although lace is now designed on a computer, and sizes and shapes are checked by laser with electronic machines, and although the stencils are traced and the pieces cut by highly perfected robots, the final adjustments always take months of trials and repeated manual intervention. The task is made more complex by the new fabrics used, which may have amazing prop-erties but are not always fully perfected. Despite the complex array of tech-

The window of the Marie Brunon store in Paris, above, where the delicate textures of lace bras and silk stockings are set off against a background of dark polished wood. A recent study has revealed that although women enjoy dreaming in front of these intimate and luxurious shops, they prefer to make their purchases in the less intimidating atmosphere of a large department store. Right, a Princesse Tam-Tam bra.

nology, when the moment comes for actually making the bra, paradoxically enough, it is little hands that must do the work, day and night fixing on a strap, braid, a bit of lace, or a fastener.

After benefiting from the cheap labor of the southern countries, manufacturers turned to Eastern Europe as a site of further factories. The Soviets, for example, had a good reputation as bra makers. They fabricated good, solid undergarments. But as with other basic products there was a shortage—sugar, meat, and bras all were scarce. A French lingerie show, organized with the cooperation of the France-USSR Council, was planned for August 1990 at the Gum department store in Moscow. Lingerie was to be sold in exchange for potash. But because of political upheavals in the USSR the event had to be canceled. Another instance of an international situation affecting lingerie was the Gulf War, which brought a downturn in fashion generally and in high-quality bras in particular. At Cadolle's, for instance, the great majority of its wealthy American clientele declined to buy luxury lingerie.

The Bra Museum in Los Angeles, below, where one can view the undergarments of some of Hollywood's greatest stars. In the photograph are those of Zsa Zsa Gabor, the onetime Miss Hungary, whose arrival in the United States proved a boon to gossip columnists. Bottom, the giant bra in Woody Allen's *Everything You Always Wanted to Know About Sex** (1972), designed to catch a pair of runaway breasts.

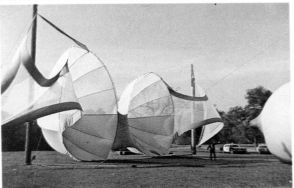

More and more brands of bras are being sold in large department or discount stores, where young women can buy them for under twenty dollars, sometimes without even trying them on. The selection offered is enormous, and these women are not as demanding as older consumers—many of whom remain faithful to specialized lingerie stores.

At the other extreme are a new generation of stores that are more intimate and luxurious, where all the styles are displayed on hangers. A precursor of this type of store was the Paris boutique Sabbia Rosa, which was decorated like a small theater in velvet and mirrors—a real boudoir. The success of the Victoria's Secret chain stores and mail-

The figure analyzer, right, developed by the Japanese lingerie manufacturer Wacoal. The shopper can see on the screen how different underwear would correct her physical imperfections. Until the 1950s, the traditional ideal for the Japanese woman was a tubular figure, and a sort of cushion was used to hide any indentation at the waist. As fashions grew more international, however, Japanese women started to favor a more defined silhouette. The Wacoal Company, founded in 1950, set itself the goal of becoming the global leader in fifty years. In 1980, the company was making its first inroads into the United States; ten years later it penetrated the European market.

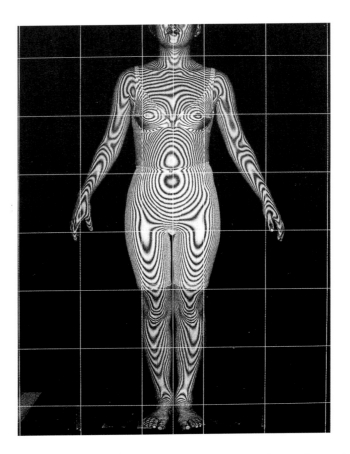

order business suggests that lingerie continues to be a booming business. American women on average buy four or five bras a year.

On the global scale lingerie is, for all its intimacy, a market fought over by men in business suits. After having bought Dim, the American Sara Lee group acquired Playtex in 1991 and became the world leader in lingerie, ahead of Triumph, the German firm, and Wacoal, from Japan. Sales figures aside, the prize for novelty bras undoubtedly goes to the Japanese subsidiary of Triumph that commemorated the bicentennial of Mozart's death with a musical bra. Thanks to its electronic chip, every time this bra is fastened it plays one of the great composer's melodies.

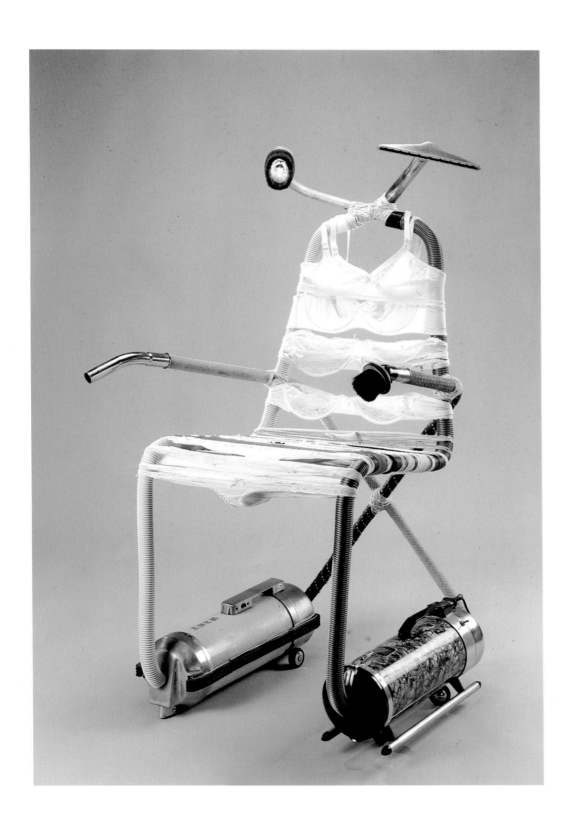

Bergère, a sculpture by the artist, poet, and furniture designer Radjar Coll-Part, is composed of vacuum cleaners, steel tubes, women's underwear, and a halogen lamp. Photograph by Roland Menegon, from *Quelle horreur!*, published by Syros Alternatives. Overleaf, the Atlas and Reggi-Netto bras by the Italian designer Giuseppe Di Somma. The bra, in Dadaist fashion, has become an object of absurdity.

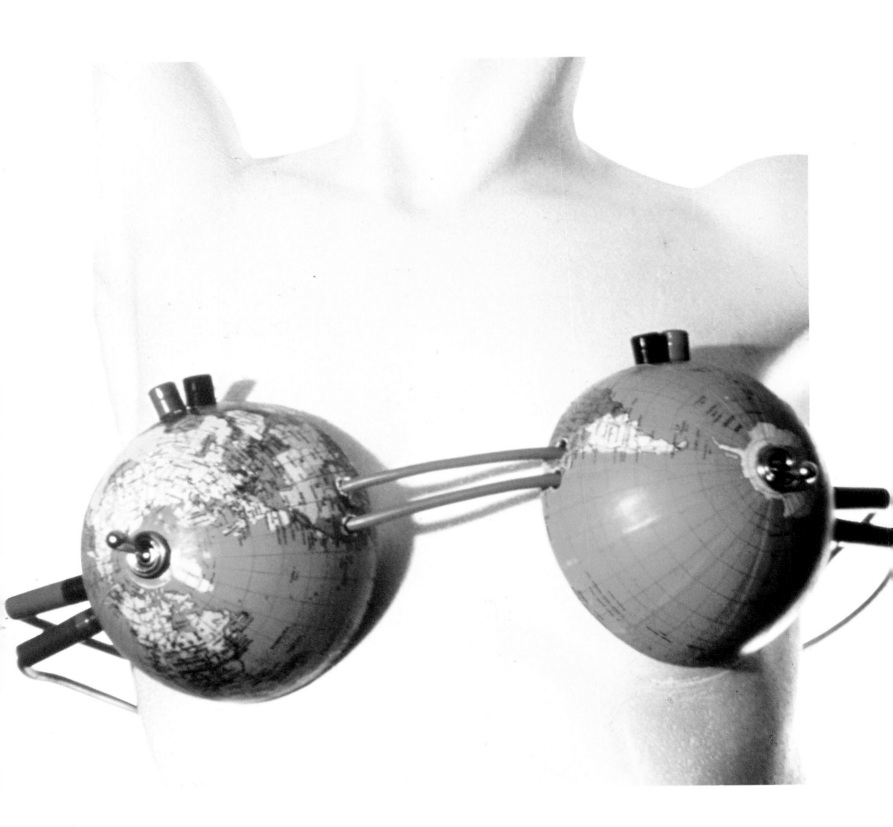

EPILOGUE

Squashed breasts, pinched waists, restricted breathing, inverted nipples, arched backs—this is but a brief catalogue of the forms women's bodies have taken, from the rounded bellies of the Middle Ages to the pert bottoms on the streets of Paris or New York, in feeding the phantasmagoria of the human imagination.

Women burned their bras in heated rebellion in 1968. Ten years earlier, Marilyn had put hers in the refrigerator, in Billy Wilder's *Seven Year Itch*, to provide coolness during a heat wave. The most poetic image of a bosom is one reported by Théophile Gautier, of a young Roman woman buried under the lava of Mount Vesuvius in A.D. 79. Nothing is left of her but the mold of one breast, "a bit of coagulated black ash, looking like a fragment from the mold of a statue broken during casting; the practiced eye of the artist can easily recognize in it the lines of a shapely breast and a rib cage in the pure style of a Greek statue. . . . Thanks to an eruption that swiftly destroyed four towns, this noble form—whose original turned to dust almost two thousand years ago—has survived. The curve of a breast has come down through the centuries intact, when so many empires have disappeared without a trace."

Despite exceptions during certain historical periods—the Roaring Twenties comes to mind—women have generally emphasized their breasts. What meaning are we to draw from the revealing necklines and rounded breasts found

Her eyes seem to look into eternity. A small female statuette with a child's face and breasts like shiny horns, she is so beautiful, so arresting, she pierces the heart (Fang art, Gabon, Musée Dapper, Paris). Overleaf, the mermaid has gone back into the ocean, leaving her straw bra on the beach (Dolce and Gabbana, featured in *Marie-Claire Bis*, summer 1992).

throughout history? Dr. Gros, in his history of the breast, offers a bold ethnographic theory that bluntly equates women of the 1990s with their prehistoric forebears. According to Dr. Gros, breasts that are made to bulge artificially (with underwire bras, for example) constitute "optical sexual signals." Roundness, which is most typical of young women, becomes particularly pronounced at ovulation. Swelling breasts, therefore, coincide with the optimal conditions for procreation. Dr. Gros suggests that today the breasts are a substitute for the buttocks as an essential sexual stimulant (the poet Verlaine, in fact, called the buttocks "the breasts' big sisters"). This would explain their irresistible attraction. Are swollen breasts another incarnation of the Venuses of prehistory, whose clusters of rounded forms were signs of fertility? Confronted with the clueless and terrifying mysteries of life, humankind protects itself with magic symbols. The art historian Hubert Comte, describing the Venus of Lespugue, offers an insight: "This small female shape still moves us after so many millennia, offering a prayer that the chain of generations not be broken! She does not represent Venus but one of those mother-goddesses present in so many cultures, the mother of mothers, whose memory slumbers in all women, as in all men, much like the precious image of Eve herself."

SELECTED BIBLIOGRAPHY

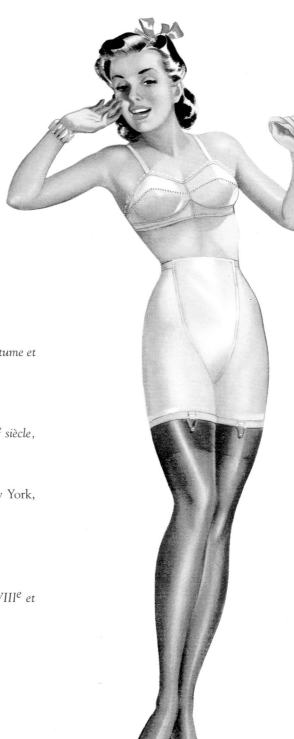

Aymé, Marcel. *La Jument verte*, Paris, 1933.

Boileau, Jacques. *De l'abus des nudités de gorge*, Brussels, 1675.

Bologne, Jean-Claude. *Histoire de la pudeur*, Paris, 1986.

Borel, France. *Le Vêtement incarné, les métamorphoses du corps*, Paris, 1992.

Boucher, François. *20,000 Years of Fashion*, expanded ed., New York, 1987.

Burgelin, Olivier, and Philippe Perrot, eds. *Parure, pudeur et étiquette*, Paris, 1987.

Comte, Hubert. *A la découverte de l'art*, Paris, 1978.

Debay, E. *Hygiène et physiologie du mariage*, Paris, 1861.

Delumeau, Jean. *La Civilisation de la Renaissance*, Paris, 1967.

Ewing, Elisabeth. *Dress and Undress, A History of Women's Underwear*, New York, 1978.

Faure, Elie. *Histoire de l'art*, Paris, 1909–21.

Gaches-Sarraute. *Le Corset, étude physiologique et pratique*, Paris, 1900.

Juvernay, Pierre de. *Discours particulier contre les femmes débraillées*, Paris, 1635.

Kybalova, Ludmila; Olga Herbenova; and Milena Lamarova. *Encyclopédie illustrée du costume et de la mode*, Paris, 1970.

Laurent, Jacques. *Le Nu et le dévêtu*, Paris, 1979.

Léoty, E. *Le Corset à travers les âges*, Paris, 1893.

Libron, Fernand, and Henri Clouzot. *Le Corset dans l'art et les moeurs du XVIIIe et XIXe siècle*, Paris, 1932.

Martin, Richard, and Harold Koda. *Infra-Apparel*, New York, 1993.

Milbank, Caroline Rennolds. *New York Fashion, The Evolution of American Style*, New York, 1989. Reprint, 1996.

Montreynaud, Florence. *Le XXe siècle des femmes*, Paris, 1989.

Ohara, Georgina. *The Encyclopedia of Fashion*, New York, 1986.

Perrot, Philippe. *Les Dessus et les Dessous de la bourgeoisie*, Brussels, 1984.

Perrot, Philippe. *Le Travail des apparences ou les transformations du corps féminin aux XVIIIe et XIXe siècles*, Paris, 1984.

Racinet, Albert. *Histoire du costume*, Paris, 1880.

Saint Laurent, Cecil. *A History of Women's Underwear*, London, 1986.

Silvestre, Armand. *Les Dessous à travers les âges*, Paris, 1911.

Witkowski. *Tétomania*, Paris, 1898–1907.

PHOTOGRAPH CREDITS

Archiv für Kunst und Geschichte, Berlin: 9, 11r., 20, 21, 26, 33, 68, 97, 98, 99, 100. **Archives Larousse-Giraudon:** 90, 95. **Aubade:** 122, 123, 127. **Bibliothèque des Arts Décoratifs, Paris, photos Jean-Loup Charmet:** 18, 19, 30t., 31, 32, 37, 38, 42, 45, 47, 48, 49b., 49r., 52, 53l., 54, 58, 60, 61, 62t., 66, 69, 70, 71, 74, 80, 86, 101, 104, 105r. **Bibliothèque Forney, Paris:** 63l., 64, 65, 115l., **Bibliothèque Nationale, Paris:** 72. **Bridgeman-Giraudon:** 14, 83. **Bulloz:** 15, 24, 28, 30b., 40t., 44. **Cadole:** 75. **Jean-Loup Charmet:** 96. **Christophe L.:** 145, 151b. **Coll. part., photo Roland Menegon:** 153. **Dagli Orti:** 12–13. **De Selva-Tapabor:** 59, 105l. **Dim, photos Peter Lindberg:** 133, 134. **D.R.:** 132. **Edimédia:** 36. **Explorer Archives/FPG International:** 88, 109l., 126. **Giraudon:** 8, 11l., 16, 17, 23, 25, 27, 34, 35, 41, 43, 46, 56–57, 79. **Harlingue-Viollet:** 84l., 93. **Huit:** 135, 136. **Hulton-Deutsch Collection, London:** 55, 81l., 85r., 87, 107. **Keystone:** 76, 82, 85l., 106, 115r., 124b. **Keystone-L'Illustration:** 92, 94. **Kharbine-Tapabor:** 89, 121t., 125. **The Kobal Collection, London:** 5. **Lili Cube:** 138. **Magnum:** 112bl., 113br. **Marie-Claire:** 128, 129, 150r. (photo Gearon). **Marie-Claire Bis (photo Moser):** 158. **Hervé Morvan "Les Virtuoses de la réclame," Paris:** 4, 159. **Thierry Mugler:** 143tl., 143br., 147tl., 147bl. **Musée de la Bonneterie, Troyes:** 49t., 53r. **Musée Dapper, Paris, photo Gérald Bergonneau:** 157. **Musée de l'Homme, Paris:** 10r. **William Pac:** 150t. **Alain Pelé:** 108, 108r., 110, 111, 116, 117, 118, 121b. **La Perla:** 149l. **Photothèque de la Cinémathèque française:** 112–13b., 113tr. **Playtex:** 130, 131. **Princesse Tam-Tam, photo Gilbert Benesty:** 142. **Réunion des musées nationaux:** 6, 29, 39, 40b., 40–41, 63r., 67, 78, 80r., 84r. **Roger-Viollet:** 91, 120, 124t. **Scala, Florence:** 10l., 22, 50–51. **Stills:** 146, 147br. (photo Arnal-Garcia), 151t. **Stills-Pelé:** 112tl., 112–13t. **Chantal Thomass:** 139r., 140, 143tr. (photo Guy Marineau), 143bl., 148. **Wacoal:** 152.

ACKNOWLEDGMENTS

For their confidence, help, and advice, the author would like to thank:
Emmanuelle Bernheim, Françoise Chaze, Jean-Claude Forest, Anne Hübrecht,
Catherine Klein, William Pac, Magali Roux.

BOOK DESIGN

Catherine Le Troquier

ENGLISH-LANGUAGE EDITION:

Project Manager: Ellen Rosefsky Cohen
Editors: Beverly Fazio Herter, Elisa Urbanelli
Design Coordination: Dirk Luykx and Tina Thompson

Library of Congress Cataloging-in-Publication Data
Fontanel, Béatrice.
[Corsets et soutiens-gorge. English]
Support and seduction : a history of corsets and bras / by Béatrice Fontanel ;
translated from the French by Willard Wood.
p.   cm.
Translation of: Corsets et soutiens-gorge.
Includes bibliographical references (p.).
ISBN 0–8109–4086–8 (clothbound)
1. Corsets—History.   2. Brassieres—History.   I. Title.
GT2075.F3613   1997
391.4'2—dc21   97–14551

Harry N. Abrams, Inc.
100 Fifth Avenue
New York, N.Y. 10011
www.abramsbooks.com